fractured

A Story of Broken Ties

a novel by

Renee Propes

The Kimmer Group

The Kimmer Group
Publisher's Note: This is a work of fiction. Names, characters, places, and incidents are a product of the author's imagination. Locales and public names are sometimes used for atmospheric purposes. Any resemblance to actual people, living or dead, or to businesses, companies, events, institutions, or locales is completely coincidental.

Cover and Design-Aaniyah.Ahmed

Fractured-A Story of Broken Ties/Renee Propes – First Edition
ISBN 978-1-7348219-4-9 (PB)
     978-1-7348219-5-6 (HB)

Library of Congress Control Number:2020111019

To my husband, Hardy – who is my greatest inspiration and who taught me the art of acceptance

August 1977

The five-mile warning for her exit came sooner than she expected. Too soon. A bubble of panic rose in her throat. Was she really ready to have this conversation?

She pulled off the interstate to put on her makeup. It was a regular occurrence since becoming a mother. As she looked into the mirror, she applied mascara and wiped her face with a light moisturizer before dabbing her lips with a neutral shade of lipstick.

He once said that he had fallen in love the very first time he saw her. He loved her intoxicating and exotic appearance, her model figure, and her smooth olive complexion. But the features he found most attractive were her dark, soulful eyes and her raven hair.

She pressed her foot to the accelerator and glanced at the clock on the dashboard. Somehow, she'd missed most of the three-hour drive north on Interstate 85. She glared at the signpost announcing the approaching exit, as if it were somehow responsible.

Her gaze darted to the rearview mirror as her baby boy whimpered and tugged at one ear. His little cheeks looked flushed. Teething, she guessed. Or maybe he was picking up on her own anxious tension. His eyelids drooped.

She pulled her gaze back to the road.

What was that street address again?

1

With shaking hands, she reached for the envelope she'd scribbled the address on earlier that morning. She wondered if she was doing the right thing.

Was it ever a good idea to manipulate someone's life?

But she wasn't really manipulating. She was giving the man she loved a chance to meet his son.

Sensing the silence from the backseat, she stole another glance in the rearview mirror and sighed. Her precious son had finally drifted off to sleep. How many times during the last twelve months, had she imagined who her baby might grow up to be? She'd dreamt of the rich, rewarding life he might have, now that she was free of her family's business?

She smiled. She could give him that life. *They* could give him that life starting today, if all went well. How could anyone look at that adorable face and not fall completely in love?

At the end of the exit ramp, she peered from right to left. Which way? The road to the right seemed to narrow, while off to the left, a pale shape, like the top of a skyscraper, rose over the trees. Left, she decided, and turned onto the divided highway. A few minutes later, she sighed with relief as a colorful, oversized billboard greeted her. Welcome Home! You are now in **Abington, Georgia**.

The street signs marked the route into the small southern city as she drove toward the center of town. Straightaway, she recognized his white, 1960 Chevrolet Corvair, in the parking lot of an office building just off the town square. Looking around for a better view of the building, she parked across the street.

The car suddenly felt too hot. She lowered the car window and took a deep breath. The shaking eased a little as she ran her hand through her hair. Above the sounds of the city traffic, someone blew a horn. Her baby let out a fussy little whimper and strained against the straps of his car seat.

"It's all right," she crooned. "It's all going to be fine."

The office building's front door flew open and there he was, the man she'd come to see.

She smiled.

He moved with such ease. There was that crooked little smile, and that unruly lock of hair she loved to push back from his forehead. And that gait. She used to stand at the window and watch him walk to his car when he left her apartment each night.

Thoughts spinning, she stumbled from the car and walked around to remove her son from his car seat. Her stomach did a little flip, as she mentally rehearsed the speech she'd practiced in front of the mirror.

With her hand still on the door handle, she glanced back toward the building. He still stood on the steps, smiling over his shoulder as the door opened a second time. A petite blonde joined him.

The perfect girlfriend. She had it all, the long, sleek, cornsilk-colored hair, and the excellent Aryan features. And, of course, the designer dress belted tight across her *flat* stomach.

Her eyes stung.

While she watched, he cupped his hand beneath the woman's chin and gave her a familiar kiss.

The same way he kissed me many times.

He pulled away and gave the woman a loving look. That, too, was the same.

She steadied herself against her car as the man she loved walked down the steps, hand in hand with another woman.

The wedding ring on her left hand sparkled. Then, the world around her disappeared as she processed the reality of the moment.

Of course, she was the perfect American trophy wife, with her dazzling smile and that flawless alabaster skin. She looked at her own reflection in the window, as she ran her fingers through her jet-black hair and compared her medium skin tone.

She turned and walked back around to the driver's side of the car. She couldn't do this to him.

He's made his decision.

She got back into the driver's seat, and headed out of the parking lot. Funny how things could change, she thought, her gaze wandering toward her baby in the rearview mirror.

As she left the charming town, she reflected on one recurring thought: A *life-altering decision took only a split second, but* broken ties could last forever.

Chapter One

(February 2014)

Laura Whelchel stood in front of the dining room window of her stately home and gnawed at her lower lip as her friends pulled into the circular driveway. Her chic blonde hair was styled in a mid-length bob, and her dress was impeccable.

Looking out over the pasture across the road, the black clouds began to clear the sky. It was like the moving clouds opened a curtain on Broadway and the sunlight peeking through was the promise of a magnificent performance.

As her friends got out of their vehicles, they waved to each other like excited schoolgirls as they scurried around to remove the dishes of food they prepared for her dinner. The scene was an academy award-worthy performance. They blew air kisses to each other, careful not to disturb their freshly applied lipstick.

Laura shook her head. *Look at them, laughing and joking as if they aren't visiting a friend in mourning.*

They were acting as if nothing had changed, yet Henry's death had turned everything in Laura's world upside down.

That was me just one week ago.

What a fake she was driving around in her sleek SUV, dressed in expensive designer clothing, delivering elaborate dishes of food prepared by someone other than herself to people throughout the community.

Laura lowered her head, shameful for passing judgment on her friends.

She murmured with slight justification, "But that was last week."

Her husband, Henry Whelchel, a partner in the prestigious law firm of Byrd, Whelchel & Byrd, was a renowned criminal attorney during the early years of his career. Later, he became well known for helping hundreds of clients with tax planning until the end of his lengthy career.

But now, two months shy of his 65th birthday, he was dead. A sickening feeling came over her. She wondered if Henry had adequately provided for her future needs. Laura's heartbeat quickened as it occurred to her she might not be able to afford the expenses of maintaining the plantation-style home and the forty-four acres on which it stood.

Perhaps she would need to sell the pearl-white Cadillac Escalade Henry gave her two years earlier before they learned that cancer had invaded his body. He joked and said as he handed her the keys, "This, my dear, is my parting gift to you."

The remark seemed innocent at the time, but now her stomach churned at the reality of the situation.

Laura turned from facing the large ceiling to floor window. Smoothing her skirt, she prepared to greet her friends as they approached her front door.

She passed the bounty of food already displayed on the mahogany table when Claire walked into the dining room with another platter of fried chicken. Walking toward the foyer, Laura paused. She looked at the large platters of food on the table.

How could anyone eat at a time like this? I never knew how paralyzing grief could be. It's challenging just to get out of bed in the morning and painful to put one foot in front of the other.

When she looked up, she glanced into the kitchen where the wives of Henry's business partners, and her friends, Claire Williams and Daisy Byrd sat. They were cataloging dishes into a computerized template she designed many years ago. Friends had been dropping off food since the early morning hours, like a steady stream of items rolling from an assembly line.

During Henry's hospitalization, her friends remained by her side, each one taking turns staying the night with her. They took care of her every need, scheduling appointments and driving her to get her hair done and to meet with the minister. Laura was grateful for their thoughtful suggestions while she made the arrangements for a funeral worthy of her husband's professional position.

Although Henry had been a simple, unpretentious man, it would please him to know the care she had taken to plan his Celebration of Life service.

Daisy and Claire insisted Laura keep the family informed of her decisions regarding the minister and the individuals she asked to speak at the funeral. She prepared for an elaborate, open-bar buffet at the Club following the service.

Should I have planned a smaller reception at the church instead?

As she walked toward the front door, maybe out of habit, she stole a glance at herself in the mirror hanging above the marbled-top table, in the foyer. Someone, perhaps Claire, who was the interior decorator of the group, combined several flower bouquets into one massive vase and placed it on the tabletop. Laura paused and appreciated the beautiful display, filled with various colors of flowers and a variety of greenery. It was unlike anything she had ever seen.

"Claire sure has a flair for dramatic design," Laura said.

"Did you call for me, darling?" Claire rushed to her side. "Please, sweetie, go into the parlor and sit while we handle the visitors. You shouldn't concern yourself with greeting friends at the door."

When she heard the doorbell, she dreaded making conversation with her excitable friends as she walked to the parlor and found a comfortable chair.

While touching the large stone that sat upon the gold ring on her left hand, she placed her feet on the ottoman.

Then, she overheard Claire say, "Missy, darling, someone's at the front door."

As she looked around the room, she realized that she'd sat in the parlor only twice during the time they lived in the house. Both times involved unexpected visits from nervous young men to ask her and Henry for permission to marry their daughters.

Laura looked up to see the mayor's wife, Delores Levinson, standing in the foyer, holding an angel food cake and a Tupperware bowl filled with fresh sliced strawberries. Delores was the last person Laura wanted to see because of what Henry had gone through with her family.

Claire spoke to Delores and directed her to the kitchen. Then she returned to the parlor to check on Laura.

"Please, Claire," Laura raised an eyebrow. "Can you handle the visitors tonight while I go into my bedroom and hide under the covers until this is over? I'm just so tired, and I don't have the energy to face anyone else today."

"Now, you just sit here while I go into the study and get you a drink of bourbon from Henry's private stock. I'm sure he wouldn't mind sharing a drink with his bride."

Not long after Laura finished the bourbon and retired, her three daughters began to arrive for the weekend leading up to their father's memorial service on Sunday afternoon.

Chapter Two

B etsy, the youngest daughter, and the one Henry had worried about most, arrived soon after seven o'clock with her husband, Hal, and their two boys, Rob and Daren. It was apparent the Carpenter family did not weather the two-hour trip well.

As soon as Hal cut off the engine, Betsy jumped out of the car.

Her family lingered behind.

As usual, Betsy wore her long blonde hair pulled back in a ponytail which was a smart look for her. Her small, petite body moved quickly as she stormed into the house with the force of a cyclone. Unlike her husband and boys, she was on a mission.

While she looked around for her mom, she knew her childhood home had changed. The structure and location were the same, but she sensed a profound void.

The atmosphere inside the once cheerful home was not the same as the last time she visited her parents. First, the aroma of fresh flowers was overwhelming, and there was also a stench of burnt coffee in the air. As she walked through the kitchen, there was an empty coffee pot sitting on the silver Mr. Coffee machine's plate. If it had continued unnoticed, the glass would have shattered from the stress of the extreme heat. It was apparent her mother was not in control of her

9

household now, so Betsy looked around for the person whose charge it was to keep things in order.

When Betsy walked through the dining room, she spotted Claire and Daisy talking with a group of ladies in the parlor, but when she walked into the room, they stopped talking. Claire looked over and said, "Betsy, darling, I'm so sorry, my dear, we didn't hear you come in. Where are the boys, did they come with you or are they coming later with Hal?"

"No problem… the boys are in the kitchen with Hal looking for snacks." Betsy looked around the dining room at the lavish display of food, and although she couldn't eat a bite, she realized her children were hungry.

"Where is my mom?"

"Honey, your mom was tired, so we gave her a sip of hot toddy about an hour ago and put her to bed. She will feel better after a good night's rest. But let's get your family into the dining room and feed those growing boys of yours." As Claire put her arm around her, Betsy realized she had not shed one tear since coming into the house.

"I want… no, I need to see my mother. Claire, would you please help Hal and the boys to some supper while I slip into Mom's room for a few moments?"

"Of course, honey. You go on in and visit with your mama."

She hugged Claire. "Thanks."

Betsy went toward the master suite at the end of the house and stopped outside her mother's door. Hearing no sounds, she knocked softly.

"Come in."

She turned the knob gently and then peeked through the opening. Her mother was in bed, her head covered by the duvet.

"Mom, are you okay?"

"Yes, dear, I'm just a little tired from all the activity this week. But I'll be fine in the morning."

Betsy knew she should probably hug her Mom, but there was something she needed to get off her chest. She'd spent the two-hour trip rehearsing what to say, and she wasn't about to let the momentum slip away.

"Well, I need to talk to you about the service on Sunday. I think Hal should be the one to deliver the family eulogy since he's the only son-in-law. Besides, Hal felt a particular closeness to Dad after losing his father last year."

Laura threw back the covers and sat up in the huge king-size bed. Betsy sat down in the Queen Anne chair next to the picture window and watched her mother place the pillows behind her back.

"Honey, perhaps you're not aware, but your father left me detailed instructions about his funeral. Tomorrow, I plan to show you and your sisters the letter he left me, and I'm counting on you to help carry out his wishes."

"Mom, you don't understand, I need Hal to speak at the funeral. It doesn't matter what Dad wrote on a piece of paper ten years ago. Hal needs to speak, period. Do you understand?"

Smiling, her mother patted the covers on the bed. "Come over here, sweetheart. I need a hug from my beautiful daughter."

Betsy bit her bottom lip and turned her head to the window, pretending not to hear her mother's request. When she looked back at her mom, there were fresh tears in Betsy's eyes, and her bottom lip quivered.

"Do you want to talk about it, sweetheart? Perhaps the timing isn't perfect, but we are in the same room, with nothing but air between us. So, if you want to tell me what's going on, I'm ready to listen."

Betsy sobbed. Laura got up from her bed and walked over to her daughter and said, "Okay, little girl, you got me out of bed. So spill it."

Suddenly, the door swung opened, and Julia came into the bedroom.

"Hello, Julia… When did you get here, honey?" Laura asked as she met her middle child with a hug.

"We just pulled in, and Claire told me you two were in here chatting, so I came on in." Clinging to her, she looked from her mother to her younger sister.

"Are you two okay?" Julia asked.

Laura sighed. "As well as expected, considering we lost a husband and a father yesterday morning." She glanced over at Betsy and said, "isn't that right, sweetheart?"

"Yeah, tell me about it," Betsy said. "Who knew the death of a parent would be so traumatic? It isn't like his death should be a surprise, right?"

Betsy got up from the chair and wiped the tears from her face.

"I'm going to the kitchen to check on the boys and get a Diet Coke. Do either of you want anything?"

Her mother glanced at her with an apologetic smile.

"No, sweetheart, I'm fine."

When Betsy left the room, she slammed the bedroom door behind her.

Laura closed her eyes and held them shut. Because she was the youngest, Laura expected Betsy to take her dad's death the hardest. The name Betsy meant "God is my Oath". Ironically, Henry had chosen the name for their youngest child.

Julia scrunched her nose and managed a sympathetic smile as she ran her fingers through her long, blonde hair. "It seems like Betsy is in rare form tonight."

Laura forced a smile. "Yeah, well, grief is a cruel form of education. It brings out the worst in some folks, while others can handle it with grace. But as we know, our Betsy never handles adversity with grace."

Julia did not respond.

"Now, tell me who came with you tonight? When you first came into the room, you said that we just drove up. Who were you referring to?"

"His name is Fitzgerald Romano. Now that we're here, maybe this isn't the best time to introduce my friend to the family. I thought having everyone together this weekend would make it easier. But I wish now we had come home last weekend so Dad could have met him. Dad would have loved him. In fact, Mom, Fitz reminds me of him in so many ways."

"Well, sweetheart, you know what they say. Girls search for men like their dads. When I met your dad, he had some of the same attributes as my father, and I'm certain that's why I married him."

"Do you mind if he comes in for a few moments so you two can meet?" Julia asked.

"Sweetheart, I'm looking forward to meeting your friend. But tonight isn't the time and my bedroom isn't the place. I have smiled and engaged in small talk since early this morning, and I don't have the energy now to play the gracious hostess to your friend. However, if you will allow me the pleasure of a good night's rest, I promise to meet him first thing in the morning." Laura smiled at her daughter.

She turned to her nightstand and grabbed the cup of bourbon and ginger ale Claire gave to her earlier in the evening. Looking inside the empty cup, she said, "I wonder what time your older sister will get here?"

Julia turned her head as if she heard a noise, then said, "Sounds like she just arrived." She cracked the door and listened for her sister's voice. Turning back to her Mom, a gigantic smile appeared on her face when she said. "Here she comes."

From the sitting area outside the master suite, Laura could hear Marsha saying, "How are you, Julia? I'm so glad you're here."

Marsha grabbed her sister when she entered the room and sobbed. "Oh, Julia, why couldn't we have just one more weekend together as a family? What I wouldn't give to hear his contagious laugh, and listen to one more of his amusing stories. And to experience the love that showed through his soft brown eyes. You know what I mean, don't you? Daddy said more with those beautiful eyes than he could ever tell us in words. He could just look at me and smile, and I knew his heart was sending me a blessing."

"I know, right?" Julia said. "But his eyes could also convey the same level of disappointment. In fact, it was awful being on the receiving end of those stares."

"Everyone knows I never disappointed Daddy," Marsha said. "I was the firstborn, and he gave me his strong leadership and diplomatic skills, along with this beautiful dark hair and his flawless olive complexion," She stated in jest as she patted her own face.

Julia lifted her hand in the air and said, "Yeah, I know. I've heard that throughout my entire life. You were the firstborn, and Betsy was his baby!"

Marsha looked at her mother, knowing that Julia had touched a nerve.

"Mom, how are you?" she said as she hugged her.

"I'm okay."

"As usual, you are a tower of strength, and so put together. Look, not a hair out of place…" Marsha said. "Mom, you look beautiful in those silk pajamas. That shade of turquoise looks great with your blonde hair and blue eyes,"

"Well, honey, it's because I plastered my hair in place with hairspray. Tomorrow, I'm going to J. Green Salon for a shampoo and blowout. Jane's agreed to meet me at nine o'clock in the morning. I told her that I just didn't have the energy to do it myself."

Marsha hugged her mom again before releasing and said, "Speaking of Betsy, she didn't look too good when I walked through the kitchen. She's got poor Hal cornered with her finger in his face. What's up with them? Is there trouble in paradise, or what?"

Laura raised her eyebrows. "Something's up all right, but I'm not sure what it is. As soon as she got here tonight, she started talking about Hal delivering the family eulogy. She all but demanded that he do so."

Marsha looked at Julia. "Mom, we are okay with that decision, if you are. Hal's an impressive guy and he's an excellent public speaker, so he would be the perfect choice."

"Thanks for that vote of confidence for your brother-in-law, but your father left a letter with complete instructions detailing his memorial service. I feel it my obligation to honor his last wishes."

"Well, of course, Mom," Marsha said as she glanced at Julia. "We'll honor his request. Who did he name as the eulogist for the family?"

"He chose you, Marsha," Laura said. "And you must admit, you're the only one of us who can stand in front of your father's friends and peers and speak without breaking down. You were born with that determined resolve to get through awkward situations with unyielding grace. Please don't argue with me about this, honey. Had Henry wanted Hal to deliver the family eulogy, he would have told me. He wanted you, Marsha, our firstborn child."

Julia winked at her sister, "Oh, the honor of being the firstborn child of Henry and Laura Whelchel."

Laura turned to Julia and looked at her with a raised eyebrow, "Well, I don't know what you are fussing about. You got the absolute best of both of us. Your father always said that you were his brainchild, the intellectual one. So, don't think you got left out by any stretch of the imagination."

Julia's eyes filled with tears as she said, "Mom, that may very well be the sweetest thing you've ever said to me. Did Dad really refer to me as his brainchild?"

"Yes, honey, he did. And he always said you were drop-dead gorgeous."

Laura then looked to Marsha. "Now, we need to discuss this situation about Betsy. I need your help to get through this complication, okay? Hal cannot deliver the family eulogy."

Laura reached for the empty cup on her nightstand and handed it to Marsha and said. "Be a sweetheart and go into your father's study and get me a drink. And get you girls one, too."

Laura went into the adjoining bathroom.

Marsha smiled and looked at her sister, and with a bit of drama, whispered, "Who knew, she's already relaxed the house rules?"

Julia looked back over her shoulder to make sure her mother was out of earshot. She rolled her eyes and mouthed, "Bring me one, too."

When Marsha returned from the study, she carried a small silver tray on which she sat her mom's coffee cup and two crystal glasses. While placing each of their drinks on a cocktail napkin, she said, "Now, before we get into another discussion, who is the gorgeous hottie sitting in the kitchen?"

Laura looked startled, "Who do you mean?"

"There is a man of apparent Italian-American descent sitting at your bar trying to eat all the food Claire has placed in front of him. He's wearing a Rolex watch, Italian leather shoes, and a custom-made suit. But he would also look fine wearing nothing at all." Marsha laughed, knowing her mother would reprimand her for her sexist description.

"Julia, is this guy your friend?"

She smiled and nodded.

"Well, drink up, girls. I need my rest if I'm to meet him first thing in the morning.

Chapter Three

A s the helicopter dropped below the morning cloud coverage, its deafening sounds interrupted the early morning stillness. The pilot circled the property that was described to him as a massive farm with dense patches of pine trees. A creek divided the farm, bounding the pasture used for the cattle, which he recognized from the sky.

He spotted the large red barn with the tin roof as the target, and as promised, there was plenty of room on the south side of the barn to land the aircraft. While circling the property, he saw the other pastures, one of which contained the horses. He counted five horses grazing in the field. As he lifted the chopper's nose and pointed the aircraft in the barn's direction he was careful not to spook the animals. He watched for signs of other livestock but saw none.

As he observed the farm's beauty and seclusion, he realized his nephew had an eye for business in discovering this property for their operation.

The massive Sikorsky S-92 helicopter was equipped with the latest technology, including advanced tracking system and satellite phone capabilities. The sophisticated phone system allowed the pilot to contact anyone in the world while supervising properties and facilitating drops from the air.

Nicolas Suarez, known to friends as Nic, engaged the phone system and spoke in a languid, but deliberate manner. "Nic here, target spotted. The scenery from up here is awesome. I'm overlooking the rolling hills of this landscape. It's covered with a blanket of ice flakes this cold winter morning."

He listened to the voice on the other end from headquarters, and then said, "Affirmative. The white cab of the eighteen-wheeler is extending from the front door of the red barn."

He listened in silence.

"It appears they're done. I will confirm and radio back in a few minutes. Stand by."

Nic smiled as he made one last sweep over the property and saw the dark brown fencing and the location of the creek, both marking the parameters.

"Yeah. Just confirmed the deposit was successful," Nic said, "and they're leaving the barn. They are now traveling the one-lane road and heading out. I'm trying to stay far enough away to not disturb anyone at the big house. So far, this morning, I've noticed no signs of movement from up there."

When Nic surveyed the property, he spotted shadows moving between the tree branches, "Correction, I am wrong about that. It appears someone is coming down the road, heading toward the barn. Both vehicles are approaching the bend in the road from opposite directions."

He quickly switched frequencies. In Spanish, Nic yelled into the device to his men on the ground, "Move over, man, you're going to hit that vehicle head on!"

He watched as the driver of the Gator continued to fiddle with something on the floorboard. When she finally looked up she was heading toward the front of the truck. She swerved to the right and barely escaped a collision.

Then, he listened to the response from the other frequency and spoke in English, "I'm on it, and I'm circling now. The vehicle is back on the narrow road and appears to be unharmed. Mission accomplished. Over."

Nic shook his fist. "You're a bunch of idiots. You'll be the death of me yet."

Chapter Four

E arly Saturday morning Laura crept into the kitchen to start the coffee, but there was a fresh pot already started. For the first time in days the house was quiet, except for the water running from the upstairs bathroom. Laura waited for the coffee to stop dripping as she looked at the clock on the coffeemaker. She had one hour to dress and get to the hair salon for a style and manicure.

While heading back to her suite, Laura thought about her girls sleeping upstairs in their childhood bedrooms. *What I would give to call my girls downstairs and crawl back into my giant bed and sleep until Monday morning. I just need my girls to be close right now.*

Later in the morning, when she returned from J. Green Salon, Laura sat down at the kitchen bar and ate a slice of the pound cake Daisy had brought over the day before. As she sipped her coffee and licked the crumbs from her fingers, she remembered her girls' homecoming the previous night.

Had Julia been ten minutes later getting here last night, Betsy would have opened up. Perhaps it's her marriage, or it could be financial worries. Still, whatever it is, I'm sure there'll be an emotional outburst soon. Henry always said that Betsy was the most transparent of the three, and the most selfish. Lord, I hope she isn't pregnant again.

And what was Julia thinking? Bringing a new boyfriend home to meet the family at a time like this wasn't a well-thought-out decision. It was so unlike her to act in such an unorthodox way. We didn't even know Julia was seeing anyone.

Laura smiled as she gathered the crumbs from her plate, licked them from her fingers, and murmured, "Goodness, this cake is so good. Of course, I haven't eaten anything since yesterday morning."

Marsha has always been like an old soul. She was always looking out for her younger sisters.

Now that Henry was gone, Laura could not allow herself to become dependent upon Marsha, but it would be hard not to. She was such a giver.

As she swallowed the last sip of her coffee, she lowered her head as fresh tears streamed down her face. "Henry, our girls need your counsel, and I need to feel your arms around me."

Laura heard footsteps on the hardwood floor, and she knew someone came into the kitchen, but her back was to the door, and she quickly wiped the tears from her face. Suddenly, someone stood at her side and gave her a light hug.

She thought it was Hal.

There was a manly scent, an expensive body wash, or cologne. But it was the Rolex watch on his wrist that told her it wasn't her son-in-law.

Laura jerked from his embrace and turned to meet the person responsible for the kind gesture, she could feel her eyes widen.

Wow, he looks like a forty-year-old version of Henry.

Laura forgot how striking Henry was back then. Perhaps his cancer aged him more than she realized.

Although his Italian ancestry was apparent, the man had the same olive complexion, the black hair with gray touches at the temples, and the same dark penetrating eyes that belonged to Henry.

She jarred herself from the daze. He was looking at her as if he could see straight through her, just like Henry so often did throughout their marriage.

"Well, hello, young man. I'm Laura Whelchel. Welcome to our home."

He smiled the most charming smile.

"My name is Fitz Romano," he said. "I was prepared to call you Mrs. Whelchel, but that sounds too old for someone as young as you. Perhaps, we can agree with Ms. Laura. What do you think?"

Laura laughed at the absurdity of the thought and said, "Laura will be fine."

"Okay, that's settled. How about a refill on that coffee? Looks like you've drained that cup."

"That would be nice. Thank you. Fitzgerald. That is your name, right?"

Like Henry, Fitz seemed comfortable with himself as he moved around the kitchen with ease.

"Yes, ma'am, but everyone calls me Fitz. I was born in America, but my families were from Colombia and Italy. My mother is Colombian, her family sent her to America during the years that President John Fitzgerald Kennedy was in office. Like most women in America, I'm assuming my mother fell in love with the charming young president. And I suppose the assassination caused his legacy to grow bigger in death than he would ever have achieved had he lived. Anyway, I'm named after him, hence the name Fitz for short."

"Nice to know the history of your name, and for the record, the story was much more enjoyable because you told it with such feeling. Where does your mother live now?"

"Thank you. My mother raised me in middle Georgia, and now she lives in Atlanta with me. Unfortunately, she has cancer and doesn't get out much."

Fitz walked to the fridge to get the creamer, and Laura saw the distinct gait. Somehow, when she saw that walk, she instinctively thought he could pass as Henry's son. He placed her cup on the counter and sat down opposite her.

Laura's hand shook as she tried to grasp her coffee cup. So, she put her hand in her lap and rubbed it.

Fitz's cell phone rang. "Excuse me, Laura, I need to take this."

"Sure, go ahead."

As he spoke into his phone in fluent Italian, she wondered about his age, but knew she would never ask. Perhaps, she would ask Julia.

Laura knew enough Italian to pick out individual words, and she could tell that he gave specific directions to a location in Georgia. Thanks to the two years of Italian she took in college, she made out enough of the conversation to know he told the caller that it was in a remote area and the property would be perfect for the operation.

When he finished with the call, he turned back to Laura without missing a beat.

"Unlike your girls, my father was never in my life. Apparently, my parents met when my mom worked as a secretary in middle Georgia. They enjoyed a brief fling, broke up, and seven months later, she gave birth to me."

"Did your father know he had a son?"

"Mom said she wrote him a letter and sent it along with a picture of me, but who knows exactly what happened?"

"Do you not believe the story your mother told you?"

"Well, I think when a single mother has an inquisitive young child, the truth possibly gets softened to avoid leaving a permanent scar on the child she loves."

Laura reached for his hand and said, "I'm so sorry, Fitz." Then, she looked at the clock.

"Thanks for coming home with Julia this weekend. I'm sure you will be a tremendous source of comfort for her."

"I'm glad I could be with her at the funeral. I know how much she loved her dad."

"I've arranged for a family meeting with my girls at one o'clock in Henry's study, so if you will excuse me, I should get ready for this meeting."

"Yes, of course. Nice meeting you."

She turned and looked at Fitz's face, and at that moment, she saw another glimpse of Henry in his smile, and the softness of his eyes grabbed at her heart.

"Please help yourself to some lunch. Ordinarily, I would prepare a nice luncheon for our guests, but this weekend we're just fending for ourselves. Fortunately, there's enough food here for everybody."

Laura turned and headed toward the study.

She sat down at the desk and breathed in the manly scent of her husband's cologne. Then she closed her eyes and leaned back in his chair.

Oh, Henry, what have you done? Mama told me years ago about a rumor she heard that you fathered a child. I should be livid, but to be honest, meeting Fitz has filled me with a peace I hadn't felt since before you passed on Thursday morning. Did you send him to comfort us?

Her thoughts traveled back in time to when she and Henry broke up for six months before they became engaged. With her eyes still closed, she did the math and determined the approximate date of Fitz's conception.

Well, whoever he is, Henry, I'm drawn to this young man, and apparently our Julia is, too. Now, I've got to get through this family meeting and then prepare for the service tomorrow.

"Hopefully, on Monday morning, I will begin to feel less like a zombie."

When she opened her eyes, Laura reached for a Kleenex and wiped the tears from her face. The girls were sitting on the sofa in front of her. Apparently, they had tip-toed into the study and overheard the last of the conversation about her feeling less like a zombie.

Laura smiled at them and said, "You should have made your presence known. I was sitting here resting my eyes and didn't hear you come in."

Then she straightened her back and placed her hands on the document they were about to discuss.

Betsy was the first to speak, "What is this meeting about, Mom?"

"Well, sweetheart, we are here to discuss your father's last wishes."

Laura paused and straightened the papers on the desk.

"Before we read through the letter, let me be clear. We prepared this letter the same weekend your father went on hospice. As you know, that was four weeks ago today. So, your father was still lucid at the time of this writing. He dictated his wishes to our attorney, Andrew Byrd, and then Andrew got someone in his office to type the document. As you will note, both Henry and Andrew signed it, and Andrew's assistant notarized the document."

Betsy stood and walked over to the desk and looked at the letter. "That's fine, Mom, but I just need to know if you will let Hal deliver the family eulogy? And I also need to know when the estate will settle because I want the house." She turned and glared at her sisters and raised her eyebrows as if to say, "So there."

Laura went to her husband's liquor cabinet and poured herself a drink.

Marsha shot a sideways glance to Julia and covered her mouth. Marsha whispered, "Mom is drinking at one o'clock in the afternoon. This isn't normal, is it?"

After Laura poured her drink, she stood in front of the liquor cabinet. She stared at the amber-colored liquid and wondered what happened to her youngest daughter since Henry's health began its steep decline.

It's only been two months.

How could anything so drastic happen to Betsy in that length of time? Obviously, she was not paying attention, because what she just heard from Betsy was a desperate cry for help.

Laura turned around and smiled, "Excuse my manners, would you ladies like a drink? I'll be happy to pour you one before we get started."

Marsha slowly raised her hand, followed by Julia. Betsy, however, did not.

Laura poured the drinks and handed a glass to Marsha.

She turned toward Julia as she held her glass and said, "Julia, I met your friend a few moments ago. I found him to be very intriguing, and I can understand your attraction to him. Here's your drink, sweetheart."

Laura touched the top of her head, and with furrowed brows, she paused, "I'll be right back."

She left the room to find her glasses. She remembered removing them when she was in the kitchen, and so, she headed in that direction. As Laura got closer to the kitchen, she overheard a conversation Fitz was having in Spanish. He was speaking in a stern and condescending tone. Disturbed, Laura stopped and listened and heard him say that the property would soon be on the market because of financial hardship. When she finally walked into the kitchen and picked up her glasses, she winked at Fitz and left without speaking a word. Although he stopped talking when she entered the room, he resumed his conversation in Spanish as soon as she was out of sight.

As Laura walked back into the study, she looked at Julia and said, "Sweetheart, what is it that Fitz does for a living?"

Julia said, "He's in sales."

Laura returned to the desk, reached for the letter, and began with a strict voice.

"Ladies, please understand, I will read this letter to you, and the four of us WILL honor your father's wishes. There will be no discussion or changes."

"And, Betsy, when the time comes for us to settle your father's estate, we will do so equitably."

She sipped her drink and said, "Now, let's begin with the reading."

Chapter Five

The ladies were all dressed in black from head to toe. At the last moment, Laura spotted a hat on the shelf in her closet, which added a look of sophistication to her simple black dress.

While standing in her dressing area, in the master suite, she looked at the full-length mirror and smiled at herself, *Henry Whelchel, I hope you were proud that you chose me for your wife.*

At one o'clock on Sunday afternoon, just one hour before the start of Henry Whelchel's celebration of life service, the girls and Laura, along with Hal, Rob, Darin, and Fitz piled into the long, white limousine that transported them to the Abington First Methodist Church.

As the limousine pulled in front of the massive rock sanctuary, the parking lot was filling up. It wasn't at full capacity yet, but people were arriving early to get a good seat.

The funeral home attendant assisted Laura as she got out of the car. He suggested they move inside to the gathering room, where they would wait until the service began.

The time seemed to stand still for Laura, as she looked at the three youthful women sitting opposite her, all impeccably dressed. Betsy sat at the end of the sofa, talking to Hal, sitting in a chair next to her.

They seemed oblivious to everyone else in the room. Marsha was reading over her notes of the eulogy she had prepared. In contrast, Julia pretended to read a bulletin and watch her mother. Fitz was on the other side of the room, with a phone to his ear while talking in an inaudible voice. She continued to watch his animated conversation.

Is it possible that he is conducting business on a Sunday afternoon? Does he never quit working?

At two o'clock, the funeral director motioned for the family to line up and go into the sanctuary. As Laura walked into the lobby of the church, she felt a hand on her elbow. Fitz was standing next to her, and his phone was no longer attached to his ear. She smiled at the kind gesture and said, "Thank you, Fitz. I'm honored for you to walk with me today."

As they entered the church, the organist was playing "A Sweet, Sweet Spirit". As the family was seated, a beautiful, soprano voice sang the lyrics of her husband's favorite hymn. Then the minister spoke for a moment and welcomed everyone to the service.

Rob, her nine-year-old grandson, walked to the podium next and read Henry's favorite scripture. Laura held her breath as his childish voice pronounced each word correctly. When Rob finished the reading, he looked out over the congregation and grinned.

It was priceless. And Henry would've loved it.

Laura glanced around the church as Marsha waited for Rob to return to his seat. And she realized every important occasion of hers and Henry's life together occurred in this very sanctuary. From the infant baptisms to their daughters' weddings, all took place in this church.

Marsha got up and moved with a quiet grace as she took her place at the lectern. It seemed her presence filled the room.

Henry, you would be so proud of Marsha. Look at her. Just like you, she's so comfortable in her own skin.

Marsha's beautiful brown eyes glistened with tears as she looked out over the congregation. With a poised voice, she began:

"*I am Marsha Whelchel, Henry Whelchel's oldest daughter. My dad requested that I deliver the family eulogy, and I consider this a great honor to fulfill his last wishes.*

"*Many of you know my father from business dealings. Perhaps you were members of the same country club or civic organization. There are at least two of Dad's childhood friends present today. On behalf of my family, we would like to thank you for taking the time to honor his life.*

"*Henry Whelchel was an exceptional individual. And, if you knew him well, you would understand what I mean. He was scholarly and kind, a rule follower, and forgiving. Still, among his many attributes, he preferred a quiet leadership style and worked well with all people. Understand, my dad majored in political science and minored in finance. He was smart and ambitious, almost to a fault. During those initial years of his career, he made a name for himself as a top criminal defense lawyer in the State of Georgia. After working fourteen, sometimes sixteen-hour days for many years, he turned his focus on tax law. Although he enjoyed representing people accused of breaking the law, his passion, he discovered midway through his career, was tax law. It allowed him to serve members of the working class as they prepared for their family's financial future.*

"*Sometimes, as a child or a young teen, my mom would drop me off at Dad's office, and he would insist I work on homework in an adjacent room. The room was not much larger than a walk-in closet. However, he had bookshelves built to store the overflow of reference books. It was in this compact room where he stored the many awards he received throughout his career. Now the awards are displayed on the bookshelves in this little alcove. But the point is my dad was a humble man, and he never wanted to bring attention to himself.*

"*I would sit in the room and listen to him talk to his clients, while pretending to complete my homework assignments. Please understand, my dad listened with his whole being. He never took notes while meeting with a client. He was attentive to their body language* and mannerisms while watching for subtle hints of information. Dad could read a person by their actions.

"As you look at his three daughters, you will note the differences in each of us. He often spoke of our differences, which he found interesting, considering we had the same parents. I always marveled at Dad's level of adaptability. He was as comfortable talking with Betsy about parenting, as he was talking with Julia about human anatomy.

"One of my favorite memories of him is a Saturday afternoon before starting to teach at the college level. We sat in his study and talked about the responsibility of being a fair professor. It was Dad's opinion that the problem with most college professors was that they taught students what to think.

"He explained to me that I should be knowledgeable on a wide range of issues, so as to encourage my students to consider all options before making an educated decision on any topic. He felt that a good formal education should teach young adults how to think for themselves and reach their own conclusions about what is important in their lives.

"My youngest sister, Betsy, is a perfect blend of Mom and Dad. It's like they apportioned their genes in equal measure for her. She has Mom's appearance, but she got Dad's passion for life. Leave it to Betsy to be the one to give Dad two grandsons as his reward for raising three daughters.

"Then there's Julia, the middle child. At first glance, she is the spitting image of our mother, until you take that second look, then you notice the warmth of Dad's eyes. Like Dad, she says more with those beautiful brown eyes than she could ever articulate with words. I've just learned that my father referred to Julia as his "brainchild." To be honest, it offended me when Mom shared this information on Friday evening. However, considering she is a nurse practitioner, I assume the title was because of all the math and science classes she took in college.

"Lastly, I am the first-born and oldest child. It's obvious that I inherited my Dad's complexion since I look the most like him. But, more than that, I have learned to persevere through stressful situations, much like my Dad has done throughout his life. He challenged me to be a better version of myself, a better student, a better citizen, even a better sister and daughter, and always treated me as his equal.

"Perhaps, it was because of his wisdom as an attorney, he could communicate his genuine feelings in any situation. He had a way of elevating everyone's self-worth, letting each think they were the most important person in the world."

As Marsha picked up her notes from the lectern, she looked tenderly down at her dad's casket.

"We're gonna miss you, Dad."

When Marsha returned to her seat, Laura couldn't stop thinking about the eulogy. Still shocked, her heart hurt that Marsha said nothing about her and Henry's relationship.

He was my husband!

She closed her eyes and wondered what her friends thought about the omission.

When the service ended, and as the family exited the church, Laura spotted Big Jim Levinson, the mayor of Abington, standing in the back row of the church. It would be hard to miss Big Jim. He was 6'5" and weighed over 325 pounds. His attendance surprised Laura because Big Jim and Henry had been through some difficult situations together. Even though Big Jim hadn't spoken to Henry for years, he and his wife Delores, came to pay their respects.

At the end of the evening, when the last of her girls left, Laura locked up the house and headed for her bedroom. She changed into her pajamas and pulled back the covers. Picking up a magazine from the side table, she crawled onto the king-size bed. Her intentions were good, possibly read a brief article and then drift off to sleep. But, as she continued to flip through the magazine, it was obvious that rest would not come easy.

She scooted down under the covers and remembered the part of the eulogy about Henry changing his focus from criminal law. As she drifted off into a world twenty years prior, she remembered the time he changed his practice from criminal law to focus on tax law.

Chapter Six

The date was Thursday, October 11th, 2001, and the year had been a troublesome one for the Abington residents. Besides the attack on the World Trade Center in New York City, there had been five unresolved murders in the town since February.

One case involved a mother and her two young children taken from their home during the early morning hours of Tuesday, February 6. There were no signs of a struggle inside the house, and there were no indications that anyone had vandalized either of the door locks or any of the windows. A jogger discovered the three bodies on Friday morning, February 9th, in a sinkhole near Hydrangea Park inside the city limits.

The second killing involved an older woman and her six-year-old granddaughter. Almost the exact profile existed between the two incidents. However, the victims of this crime took a while to surface.

The weekend following the July fourth celebration, a group of boaters pulled into Paradise Cove, preparing to enjoy a picnic, when one guy saw what he thought was a large animal trapped in a huge fishing net.

Upon examination, the guy realized he'd discovered the bodies of the woman and her granddaughter, missing since the end of April. The murderer, however, remained at large. In both instances, the perpetrator had tied the bodies together with fishing wire.

****

Laura watched as James Levinson, the sixth term Mayor of Abington, known to all in the town as Big Jim, pulled his silver Chevrolet dually into the Whelchel's circular drive.

Laura waited while her husband walked to the front of the house. "Henry, were you expecting Big Jim?"

"No. I can't imagine what would cause Jim to ride out to the farm this evening."

Henry opened the front door, and said, "Big Jim, what brings you out here at this late hour?"

The outside spotlights allowed Laura to watch as Big Jim leaned against his truck. He was wearing a navy blue Braves cap and he kept lifting it from his head and examining the white logo on the front. Although Laura didn't know the mayor well, she knew that he was a soft-spoken, gentle soul whom everyone loved and trusted.

As she stood in front of the dining-room window, she watched Big Jim remove the handkerchief from his back pocket and dab at each eye before wiping his face.

Then she heard a noise from one of the upstairs bedrooms and she turned and rushed up the stairs to make sure the girls were unharmed.

Betsy had dropped the fishbowl onto the bathroom floor and it took a few minutes to find the fish and put everything back together. Between consoling Betsy, cleaning up the water and kissing the girls goodnight, Big Jim was already gone when Laura got back downstairs.

Henry was standing in front of the kitchen sink, sipping a glass of water, when Laura walked into the room.

"What did Big Jim want?" Laura asked.

"There's been another murder in Abington. A young mother and her three daughters were found in their garage late this afternoon. The authorities haven't yet released the information to the media. But they've arrested Little Jimmy about an hour ago for murder. Big Jim is calling in all his favors to help his son. Someone allegedly saw Little Jimmy's car driving through the subdivision yesterday. They arrested him on circumstantial evidence."

"Oh, my gosh! Did Little Jimmy have an alibi?"

"Not that I know of. God only knows what happened. But Big Jim asked me to represent his son, and I couldn't very well turn him down. Besides, the fact he was one of the first people I met when I moved here, and I consider him a good friend. He has more political influence in the Georgia legislature than anyone else in the state."

Laura pulled out a stool and sat at the bar with her face in her hands. It surprised her to learn that Henry was still considering running for the Ninth District United States Congressional seat.

She was nervous for him, anxious about the whole thing. But this wasn't the time to discuss his political ambitions. *I hate to think he's serious about taking this case if he plans to run for political office.*

Laura could tell from his look that he knew she wanted to ask who it was. "It was Mrs. Henderson, over on Tupelo Drive. Charlie Henderson's family."

"Their youngest daughter, Anna Beth, is in Betsy's class. The other girls are about the ages of Marsha and Julia." She choked back tears.

"I know." Henry nodded as he walked toward the master suite.

When he returned from the bathroom, Laura was composed.

"This will be a high-profile case for you. Honey, are you sure you're up to representing the son of such a close friend?"

"You're right. It'll be all over the media. But if you could've seen Big Jim trying to hold back tears. Perhaps he needed a place to hangout for a few minutes before going home. I'm sure he dreaded telling Delores that their only child was in jail for murder. I can only imagine what he's feeling right now."

Henry grabbed his wallet and car keys and walked toward the back door. "I'm going to meet Big Jim at the jail to post bond. It shouldn't take long."

Laura followed Henry to the door, and as he opened it, she rubbed her hand on his back and said, "Honey, I understand that you must help him post bond; however, can we talk about this case when you get back? I'm not so sure we need to put the girls through another high-profile trial at their age."

"There's nothing more to discuss," Henry said. "I've already taken the case."

He kissed her cheek, walked out of the house, and closed the door behind him.

****

As Henry pulled into the parking lot at the jail, he saw Big Jim standing outside the front entrance. He parked his car, grabbed his briefcase out of the back seat, and hurried to meet his friend.

When Big Jim and Henry walked inside the lobby, several deputies greeted them. They signed in using the electronic identification system in which both were already enrolled. The Sheriff escorted them to a holding room where their meeting would take place.

As expected, Little Jimmy was indifferent about the entire ordeal. He explained that he had gone out to his campsite to prepare for a weekend bass fishing tournament, and set up the camper around 10 a.m. When he finished, he had gone back into town to purchase food and supplies for the weekend. A deputy's car pulled in behind his truck, handcuffed him, and threw him into the patrol car while reading him his Miranda rights.

Little Jimmy spent the night in jail, and the next morning at 10 o'clock, Henry Whelchel and Big Jim met at the Magistrate Court. The judge reviewed the case and determined that James Francis Levinson III, did not pose an immediate threat to himself or anyone else and was not a flight risk. He reviewed his physical and mental condition, financial resources, family ties, and criminal record.

Since there was no history of parole or probation, he passed the drug and alcohol test, and he was a lifelong member of the Abington community, they released Little Jimmy on bond. The judge found no evidence of willful or premeditated murder intent, so he followed the strict judicial guidelines and set the bail bond at $500,000.

****

In the spring of 2002, Henry was in the middle of Little Jimmy's murder trial. Perhaps, because of Big Jim's position as mayor, the case had made it on the docket much quicker than anyone expected. As the defense attorney for the case, Henry had hoped for a long wait.

He reasoned that people forgot things after a few news cycles, and a time delay would eliminate some of the community's emotions. It would be difficult for his client to receive a fair trial in the town where he grew up so soon after the murders occurred.

It also concerned Henry the jurors would be too close to the case to deliver an unemotional and unbiased verdict.

No one felt safe in their own homes, especially single mothers with young children. The attorneys for both sides argued about where to try the case because of the outrage from the women throughout the county.

The perpetrator for the two previous murder cases was still at large. The Henderson murders were discussed at every lunch counter and social event in three counties. It was the hope of the townspeople that information would be revealed at the trial to help solve the first two cases, too. One could only hope.

Due to the publicity and media circus surrounding the upcoming trial, Laura was anxious about being left at home with her young girls. Henry worked long hours, and often arrived home from the office around midnight.

To ease her anxiety, Henry purchased a sophisticated alarm system for their home and installed an electric fence around the farm's perimeter. He gave his family strict instructions to not open the door for anyone other than a family member. And under no conditions were they to answer the house phone.

As soon as the trial started, an unmarked car was parked behind their house, and another security guard positioned in a deer stand overlooking the farm. One could only describe the emotions in the town of Abington as threatening, and Henry felt it necessary to secure his own family's welfare, for him to work the hours needed to defend an accused murderer.

Laura noticed the longer Henry worked with Little Jimmy, the more convinced he was that his client was not guilty. It seemed he, too, had fallen under Little Jimmy's captivating spell.

Henry had thought many times, that James Francis Levinson III was a smooth-talking, charismatic type that could talk himself out of almost anything, including an execution.

His coal-black hair slicked back with a generous amount of hair gel, and his eyes, a piercing shade of blue, only added to his mysterious persona. He was a good-looking man, one that many women found themselves attracted to without even knowing it. He was commonly known as a womanizer. But, most people just dismissed it, because, well, "that was just who Little Jimmy was. A womanizer."

He was also an avid fisherman. Jimmy entered every tournament within a hundred-mile radius of Abington. He often pulled his camper out to the lake on Thursday after work and didn't leave the campsite until late Sunday evening. The consensus around town was that Little Jimmy's wife and daughters rejoiced to see him go each Thursday afternoon, but were deeply saddened when he returned at the end of each weekend.

Henry met only once with Little Jimmy's wife, Patsy. He decided during that interview to avoid putting her on the stand. She could not remember if her husband had come home the night before the incident occurred, and if he had, she was unclear about whether he had planned to go to work. Henry played it safe, for fear she would shed an unpleasant light on the defendant.

Henry spent long hours preparing for the trial and spent even more time prepping Little Jimmy's responses to the prosecutor's questions. Each time Henry visited him at the campsite, there was almost always a pretty young woman within the camper's periphery, but with a sideways glance or a nod of the head from Little Jimmy, the woman would disappear without notice.

The trial lasted three months. The week before delivering the closing arguments, Henry sent his client to the local tailor's shop downtown for a new suit.

****

On the night before the jurors were scheduled to render a verdict, Henry Whelchel lay in bed, unable to sleep. He watched the clock on the nightstand, as the hours slowly passed.

When Laura turned over and saw him staring up at the ceiling she asked, "Honey, are you still awake?"

He reached for her hand and said, "Yes, dear. I can't sleep."

"You've not said much about the trial," Laura said. "Did the prosecution present any evidence to prove his guilt?"

"No. That's what makes this trial so bizarre. They have nothing to prove he was even on the premises. I believe the authorities were pressured to make the quick arrest, because of the two previous unsolved murder cases. And when a neighbor mentioned seeing Little Jimmy's truck in the neighborhood, they just tracked him down and arrested him."

"Well, you're as close to the trial as anyone," Laura said. "What's your gut feeling?"

"Perhaps I'm too close."

Henry turned on the lamp and walked over to the chair in front of the bay window. "Would you mind if I make a pot of coffee?"

"Of course not. I'll go make the coffee. Would you like a piece of pound cake to go with it?"

"No. Thanks, just coffee, please."

When Laura came back into the bedroom, she carried a tray with two cups of coffee and two slices of cake. When Henry saw the cake, he looked up at her and smiled.

"You know," Laura said, "you've always said that a criminal lawyer's responsibility is not only to defend the accused, but to push the prosecutor to show proof of the defendant's involvement. Do you feel you've done your job?"

"Well, yes. I've done my job to defend my client. The prosecution hasn't proven he's killed anyone. But...."

Laura reached for his hand, "But, what, dear?"

There's something not right about this case, too many gaps in the story. And for the life of me, I cannot put my finger on it."

****

On the last day of the trial, James Francis Levinson III, walked into the Abington courthouse, looking like he had stepped off the cover of

GQ magazine. Every woman in the courtroom, and men, too, turned to look at the handsome young man as he walked to the front table to take his seat next to his defense attorney.

Laura slipped into the back of the courtroom in time to hear her husband's closing argument. Before that day, she had never been inside the Abington courthouse.

Henry wore the suit she had given to him for Christmas the previous year. It was a solid black suit, and he also wore a white dress shirt and a coordinating tie. His black shoes were shined by a professional.

When he stood to begin the closing argument, Henry cleared his throat as he picked up the shiny silver pen, which rested on the tablet in front of him.

"Your Honor. Ladies and gentlemen of the jury, you have heard the testimony of several witnesses regarding the case of the *State of Georgia vs James Francis Levinson III*. Now it is your responsibility to render justice in this case. The fate of one James Francis Levinson III rests with each of you. Mr. Levinson has a wife and three lovely daughters. He's a family man who owns an insurance company. He's at home by 6 o'clock each evening, in time to enjoy a nice quiet dinner with his family.

"Before you adjourn to decide this young man's fate. May I remind you that it is your responsibility to determine beyond a reasonable doubt that Mr. Levinson murdered Mrs. Marilynn Henderson, and her three daughters, in a willful violent act.

"It is also your duty to determine whether the State has proven beyond a reasonable doubt that Mr. Levinson murdered this loving mother and her three innocent daughters in cold blood. You need to understand the term: Beyond a reasonable doubt. This does not mean free of all doubt, but a doubt for which a reason can be given by a fair minded impartial juror upon a consideration of the evidence, or conflict in the evidence, or lack of evidence. This charge should not be entered into lightly because the future of Mr. Levinson is in your hands. A man who himself is a loving husband and devoted father to three young girls.

"Let me remind you of the fact that the State's case against Mr. Levinson is based solely on circumstantial evidence. There is no concrete proof that Mr. Levinson was present at the scene of the crime. There were no fingerprints found at the scene where the bodies were discovered or during the search of the home, which took place afterward, that linked Mr. Levinson with the murders. None. None whatsoever. There were no clothing items or any DNA evidence that even suggested that Mr. Levinson had been on the property, much less committed this horrendous crime. So, if that be the case, why is he being accused of these murders? Wrongfully accused, I might add.

"The answer to this question is simple. Mr. Levinson was wrongly accused of these murders because the State needed to solve this case as quickly as possible to alleviate the fear that our community has endured the past few months.

"It distresses me to think this young man's reputation has been irreparably damaged by this accusation for a crime he did not commit.

"Please, understand me when I say Mr. Levinson was wrongly accused of murder based on circumstantial evidence. Only because he was allegedly seen driving through the subdivision the day before the murders occurred. He drove down a public street, one many of us travel each day to avoid the downtown traffic. There was no proof presented by the State to confirm he did anything wrong. He is an upstanding young family man who attends church regularly and is at home with his family each night. Mr. Levinson was raised by doting parents in an upper-middle-class household. Although my client enjoys fishing almost every weekend, to my knowledge, that is his only fault."

The jurors deliberated for less than one hour. James Francis Levinson III was found not guilty of murder in the first degree.

On the evening of the verdict, Henry stopped by Green's and bought a bottle of champagne, and five large filet mignon steaks that had been cut fresh for the occasion. It was the middle of June, and the temperature was in the mid-seventies, which was a perfect spring evening for a cookout on the back porch with his family.

When Henry finished grilling, he allowed the steaks to rest for a few moments. He opened the bottle of champagne and handed Laura a flute as they toasted his win.

However, the celebration was short-lived.

Precisely one month later, the neighbors found Little Jimmy's wife and three daughters dead in their garage. Their bodies were tied together with fishing wire, just like the previous cases. But this time, the perpetrator left behind evidence. There was a Walmart bag left in the garage, which contained a receipt showing Little Jimmy had used his debit card to make the purchase of four rolls of fishing wire. They found black hair matching the DNA taken from Little Jimmy on the deceased's clothing and woolen fibers from a fishing jacket he was wearing at the time of his arrest.

There was a high level of alcohol found in Jimmy's body at the time of the arrest and interrogation. He began by answering their standard questions, then he told about the fight with his wife the evening of the murder. Jimmy admitted to having a drinking problem, and the more he drank, the angrier he became. While drinking, he suffered from blackout periods and could not remember where he had been or what he had done for an extended time.

During a session of continuous questioning, Little Jimmy admitted to killing his family, and was responsible for the murders in the three previous cases.

Upon hearing the news, Henry Whelchel locked himself in his office for two days. On the third day, when he emerged from behind the locked door, he told Andrew Byrd that he would change his focus to tax law. Although Henry knew the change would require a lengthy period of taking additional specialized courses, he explained he could no longer handle high-profile criminal cases.

Henry's involvement with the Levinson case ruined his suitability as a political candidate. If they had tried the case in a large metropolitan city, the outcome would have been different. But, in Abington, Georgia, where everybody knew everyone's business, Henry Whelchel's political aspirations were over.

When he got home that day, Laura saw that he was a changed man. Thanks to his previous courtroom success, he was no longer dependent upon attracting significant financial cases. And because he could set his appointments within the nine-to-five business day, he spent more time developing deep, personal relationships with each daughter.

Chapter Seven

(Two weeks after Henry's funeral)

L aura sat in the reception area of her deceased husband's law firm, waiting to meet with his partner, Andrew Byrd, about probating Henry's will. While she waited, she sorted through the mail Andrew asked her to pick up from the post office. Among the many advertisement flyers, was an envelope from the First National Bank of Abington, addressed to Mr. and Mrs. Henry Whelchel.

There was an immediate twitch in her face.

I didn't know we had any outstanding debt.

The letter stated their mortgage payment was past due. Another letter from the same bank showed that Henry had been making quarterly payments toward yet another loan.

She tossed the mail in the chair next to her and closed her eyes. Then she waited for Andrew's assistant to tell her when she could go back to his office.

"Laura," Andrew said as he hugged her, "how are you, dear?"

"I don't know, Andrew," she said as she wiped her eyes. "I've just read two letters from the First National Bank of Abington that state we are past due on loans that I was unaware existed. Do you know anything about this?"

He took the statements and gave them a quick review and said, "No, Laura, I wasn't aware. Henry and I never discussed your personal finances."

Laura handed him the stack of mail, and he scanned through the items.

"Do you know where Henry kept his life insurance policies?"

"No, I don't," she said. "Henry mentioned a policy to me about a year ago. Still, the premiums on that policy would increase at age sixty-five. It was a term policy and the premiums were steep. Henry mentioned canceling it, but I'm not sure if he did."

"Let's hope he didn't cancel that policy," Andrew said.

Andrew went over a checklist of financial statements he needed her to find. Henry had given Andrew the original Last Will and Testament to keep in the safe in his office. The document was on his desk.

She mentioned that Betsy was asking questions about the estate.

"It has been my experience," he said as he looked up from the paper, "that isn't a positive sign."

"I see you've got Henry's Will," Laura said.

"Yes. We'll need to get it probated, but first, we must file some notices in the local newspaper. Although, I need to have a better understanding of the value of the estate, at some point, we will need to meet with the girls to read the Will so they can understand the process."

"Andrew, let's hold off on talking to the girls for now."

"Well, I don't want to alarm you, but I received a phone call yesterday from Betsy's husband. You know, I've always liked Hal, but I was uncomfortable with his line of questioning about Henry's estate. Please don't mention this to Betsy just yet, but I'm concerned that he called me so soon after Henry's death."

"Goodness, I would've never guessed Hal would be that assertive. However, we may have a bigger problem than Hal."

Andrew looked over his glasses and said, "What do you mean?"

"Did you notice the guy with Julia at the funeral?"

"Yes. Fitz was his name. Right?"

"That's correct. Fitz Romano. Did you notice the similarity between him and Henry?"

Andrew's face drained of color.

"Did Fitz remind you of Henry?" Laura asked.

She watched as Andrew removed his glasses and rubbed his eyes. Laura wondered if he, too, had heard rumors about a son Henry had fathered years ago, and maybe he was trying to find a way to tell her.

"What are you getting at, Laura?"

Laura told Andrew about the conversation she had with Fitz the day before Henry's funeral. She also told him what she thought she heard him say in Italian and Spanish.

Since the funeral, Laura explained she had noticed helicopters flying low in the airspace above her farm during the early morning hours. She had also received calls from random people asking when the farm would be available for sale.

"What kind of work does Fitz do?" Andrew asked as he put his glasses back on and made notes on a legal pad.

"I'm not really sure," replied Laura. "Julia says that he's in sales, but he works out of his home. She was very vague when I asked about it."

As the meeting ended, Andrew gave Laura a list of personal items to locate to help calculate the value of Henry's estate. Andrew promised to investigate Fitz before they jumped to any more conclusions.

Chapter Eight

T he following Friday afternoon, Laura sat at the bar in her kitchen, drinking a cup of coffee while she organized the documents Andrew charged her with locating earlier in the week. She confirmed each item with a check mark. Then she checked again for accuracy. The only things missing were the life insurance policies. Laura had gone through the safe deposit box at the bank and rummaged through Henry's desk drawers and filing cabinets in the study. Still, she was unsuccessful in finding the policies.

As she looked at the completed list, she placed her hand over the stack of bank statements, a record of Henry's year-to-date retirement account, and a recap of his investment portfolio. Shaking her head, Laura thought the documents represented a lifetime of work as she meticulously put the statements in an envelope to drop by Andrew's office the next morning.

By the way, the girls are coming into town tonight... well, Betsy and Julia. Marsha had plans and couldn't make it this weekend.

Henry, maybe it's strange that I continue to talk to you as if you're still here with me. But I've depended on your excellent judgment for most of my life. Anyway, I've gotten into the habit of talking to you and it gives me a sense of peace.

Laura sealed the large manila envelope and slid it to the end of the bar. Then, as she finished her coffee, she shredded the papers she found in Henry's desk that were of no value.

"Henry, why did you hang on to every piece of paper that came in the mail? You were always so organized in your work. It surprised me to find all the trash hidden in your desk drawers."

Without warning, she looked up and Julia was standing in the middle of the kitchen with a startled look.

"Hello, darling. I didn't hear you come in."

"Mom, were you talking to Dad, just now?"

Laura laughed and cut her eyes at her daughter. "Yes, dear. Your father has been in my life off and on since high school. So, when I talk to him as if he is still here, I don't focus so much on his absence. Does that make sense?"

Julia hugged her mom and kissed her soft cheek, "Yes, ma'am. It seems you have developed a coping technique to get through the lonely days. That's a smart thing to do. You know Dad's spirit is still with us, we just can't see him in the physical sense."

Laura placed her hands on her face and sobbed.

"Go ahead and cry, Mom. That, too, is healthy for you. I'm going out to the car to get my stuff. When I come back in, we'll make some fresh coffee, and I'll tell you what I brought to cook for dinner."

Laura looked at her daughter, "Thank you, darling, I haven't even thought about dinner."

****

Julia left the kitchen, went outside to her car and opened the trunk. Then the phone rang. Her sister's name appeared on the caller I.D. She leaned back against the car and answered the call. Betsy was a high-strung individual, with a level of nervousness that seemed to register in the pitch of her voice.

Julia had called her several times since the funeral because she knew Betsy was hurting. Julia also knew Betsy would have to throw herself into her family the moment she went back home.

She opened the trunk and listened to her sister as she removed her luggage and the bags of food. Betsy told her something important had come up with her boys and that she wouldn't get there until late.

"Be a dear and tell Mom for me. I don't feel like listening to her questions about my delay."

"Sure, I'll tell her. But when has Mom ever drilled you about spending time with your children?"

"Oh, please, Julia. You know what I mean. She always asks so many questions when we talk. It's like she's keeping track of my life."

"Betsy, she's just lost her husband of thirty-five years. Perhaps she's just trying to start a dialogue with her youngest daughter. Think about it like this, Rob and Daren are probably the only areas in her life where she finds excitement. So, when you talk with her, just share as much information as you can about your boys. You'll be helping her through a hard season of her life."

"Okay, I get it. Got to go. See you late tonight - or early in the morning. Either way, please tell Mom. Love you, Sis." She hung up without allowing Julia to say anymore.

Julia drew a deep breath and slowly released it as she looked at her phone to confirm the disconnected call. And she knew her sister had not grasped what she said about their mother. She shook her head as she grabbed the bags and went back into the kitchen.

Laura hung up the phone as Julia walked inside the door.

"That was Claire," Laura said. "She sends her love."

"Listen, Mom," Julia said. "I just got off the phone with Betsy, and she's had a change of plans. She's coming, but it may be late tonight or early tomorrow morning before she gets here."

"Okay. No problem. We could just order in tonight if you like."

"How about ordering a pizza from The Pizzeria, and perhaps a small salad to go with it?"

Laura turned her head and grinned, "I was thinking the same thing. I've not had a pizza from there since the weekend you stayed with me when your dad was in the hospital. Remember, we sat in here and ate a large pizza by ourselves?"

"Yeah, I remember," Julia said with a sly smile.

"That was the last night I enjoyed a full night's rest. Perhaps it was because you were here with me. While I'm thinking about it, would you go into your father's study and look through the drawers and files? We've still not found his life insurance policies."

"I can do that," Julia said. "Have you tried contacting the insurance companies? They can tell you if the policies are still in force."

"No," Laura answered. "I haven't contacted them yet."

Julia took her bag up to her old room and then headed down to her father's study. When she walked into the room, she saw the family pictures on the bookshelf behind the desk. Julia sat down at her father's desk and began looking through the files in each drawer. The desk contained all matter of stuff from the years they had been at the farm.

She tried to open the bottom drawer, with a continual push and pull, but she couldn't get it unstuck. Then, after applying force, she pushed down on the drawer and yanked it open.

Wow! No wonder Mom couldn't open the drawer earlier.

Julia's heart raced when she saw the file with her name on it. When she opened the folder, she found every birthday and Father's Day card she had ever given to her dad. There were files for Marsha and Betsy, too.

At the very back of the drawer, she found two things: a locked metal box and a larger one that was unlocked. When she opened the unlocked box, there was a sealed manila envelope with her mother's name written on the front. Julia took the envelope into the kitchen and laid it on the bar in front of her mother.

"Mom, did you see this envelope when you were looking through Dad's desk earlier?"

Laura took the envelope from her and asked, "Where did you find this?"

"In the bottom desk drawer, there were two metal boxes. This was inside one of them." Julia watched as her mother tore into the envelope.

An enormous smile appeared on her face. "I couldn't get that drawer opened earlier. This is a policy I've been looking for. Thank you, sweetheart." She raised her hand for a high-five, "This is another example that you are the brainchild!" Laura reached over, hugged her daughter, and said, "This is cause for a celebration. Let's order that pizza and salad, and we'll have a girls' night."

After Julia called the pizzeria, she went back into her father's study, gathered some kindling, and built a fire. Then, she moved to one of the club chairs and stared into the fireplace. Of all the rooms in this beautiful home, this was the room she had loved the most. A man her age would call it their man cave, but the men from her father's generation called it a study. They'd furnished it with a mocha-colored leather sofa and two matching club chairs. There was also a beautiful mahogany desk with a piece of custom-cut glass that covered the desktop. Perhaps this was her mother's idea to prevent scratch marks from scarring the furniture.

Above the fireplace hung an oil portrait of Laura and her preteen daughters sitting around her feet. Her mom wore a beautiful white linen dress. The girls wore white outfits, Marsha wore a headband, but Julia and Betsy had sprigs of baby's breath pinned in their hair. Her father loved the picture. He used to say that God had given him charge over four beautiful angels. Tears filled her eyes as she remembered the way he looked when he glanced at the picture. It was as if he had entered a special place, a place filled with love and joy.

Laura came into the room with a bottle of wine and two glasses. "I thought I smelled a fire burning from in here," she said. "Since it's just the two of us tonight, why don't we eat in front of the fire?"

"Are you sure you don't mind?" Julia asked.

"Of course not. And if we get bored, we can watch some television."

"Please, no television. Let's just enjoy our time together, Mom."

"Thank you, sweetheart. I can't tell you how much I appreciate you coming home this weekend."

After they finished the pizza, they stayed in the study and enjoyed the fire while they talked and sipped their wine.

Laura was asleep when Betsy came in around 11:30. When she saw Betsy standing in the doorway, Julia put her finger to her lips, took the blanket from the ottoman, and draped it around her mother. Then she and Betsy went into the kitchen while Betsy ate the last of the pizza and drank a Diet Coke. She talked nonstop about the exercise class and her weekly meeting with her personal trainer.

Julia smiled, "Something has changed about you, Betsy. There is a glow about you I didn't notice when I saw you last."

Betsy smiled and shrugged her shoulders.

When Betsy finished her dinner, they locked up and went upstairs to bed.

****

Around two o'clock in the morning, Laura awoke and went toward her suite. As she passed the bottom of the stairs, she heard someone crying from a bedroom above. Laura walked up the steps and saw the door to Betsy's room was ajar, and the night light burning. She heard Betsy's voice. Whispers at first, then her voice got louder between her sobs.

"But I want to be with you forever. I want to wake up each morning, with you holding me in your arms."

Laura smiled, thinking her daughter was talking to her husband.

"No, Jack! That isn't the same. I want to wake up every morning next to you!"

Laura froze. She knew she wasn't supposed to overhear the conversation – but there she was. Laura pinched the area between her eyes, then turned and tiptoed back downstairs to her suite.

Chapter Nine

O n Saturday morning, Laura awoke to the sound of a helicopter flying overhead. Early each morning since the funeral, she had noticed more air traffic over the farm than usual. About twenty miles up the road, the military college conducted periodic training for their cadets, but this was unusual traffic even for a military exercise.

She turned on the lamp to write a note to check on the barn and the stable. About the time Henry went on hospice, he discussed with Andrew the need to hire someone to feed and tend to the horses each day. Still, Laura wasn't sure if Andrew had included checking the fencing around the farm's perimeter in the list of responsibilities. She made another mental note to ask Andrew about it when she delivered the documents to his office.

When she finished her list, Laura snuggled under the covers and remembered the phone conversation between Betsy and Jack. She wondered how they had met. But judging from the intensity of her daughter's voice the previous night, Betsy was sleeping around on Hal.

I hope she doesn't mess up and jeopardize my access to the boys.

Then, Laura remembered something Julia had said to her about the second metal box she found in the bottom drawer of the desk. Laura slipped out of bed and walked over to the study; the desk drawer was still open. The box was in the very back of the bottom drawer. She reached for it, and in an instant, remembered the small, thin key on her husband's keyring, which she carried in her pocketbook. Laura removed the box.

As she headed back to the master suite she thought that each day since Henry's death had brought yet another dilemma into her life.

When she reached the master suite, Laura quickly closed and locked the bedroom door. Somehow, she knew the contents of the box contained information that could alter her life.

Sitting in the morning's stillness, Laura heard a helicopter getting closer as it made another round over the farm. She walked over to the picture window, as she prayed the noise hadn't awakened her girls. Laura wondered why the helicopter flew over her property every morning at about the same time. She stood and watched the blinking lights on the helicopter hovering in the sky above her home as it circled the property once more, and then it flew out of view. Although it never landed, the presence of the aircraft invaded her space and interrupted her peace.

Laura turned and stared at the box she placed on the ottoman. She remembered that she needed a key to access the box, so she went into her closet and found Henry's key chain in the side zipped pocket of her pocketbook. Holding the key chain close to her bosom, she remembered the day she purchased it from Tiffany's the previous year while they were in New York City.

She rubbed the thin, gray key between her fingers as she walked back to the ottoman and sat down before placing it into the lock. Of course, it was a perfect fit, and she hesitated before lifting the lid.

"Please, let this be the life insurance policy that will allow me to stay in my home." She turned the key, and the top of the box popped open. Inside there was a manila envelope containing the letters SSR on the front. Laura rubbed her hand across the letters and then opened the envelope. Inside, she found a picture of a newborn baby wearing an infant gown and cap. Paper clipped to the back of the photograph was a copy of a birth certificate. Someone had blackened out the name of the child and the information regarding the father. Laura coughed as her heart skipped a beat.

My girls must never find this.

Her hands shook as she slid the picture and the birth certificate back into the envelope. She sealed the flap of the envelope with a paperclip. Laura soon returned to her husband's study, where she secured the metal box with the key. Then, she sat down at the desk and with extreme precision positioned the box as she had found it.

So, the rumor mill started by Mama's bridge club members was accurate.

Chapter Ten

(Flashback to 1980)

L aura loaded her station wagon with the car seat, diaper bag, and enough formula to feed Marsha during her visit. Her mother had called the night before and asked her to lunch. Laura thought something was up because her mom rarely invited her for lunch at the house. What reasoning would she have for not going to the club?

Still, remembering the discussion, her mother said, "We'll enjoy a pleasant lunch on the sunporch, and while Marsha takes her nap, we can catch up."

As soon as Minnie cleared the lunch plates from the table, her mother's mood changed. "Sweetheart," she said with a smile. "I overheard a rumor this week, and it involved Henry."

Laura rolled her eyes. "Mother, where did you hear this rumor?"

Her mother looked at her with a disapproving eye. "Let's not develop an attitude, honey. I'm trying to help you," she said. "Tuesday before our bridge club meeting, I stopped by the ladies' room to freshen up. While I was in there, Sybil and Maureen came in, too. Of course, they thought they were alone because I heard them talking in whispered voices when they opened the door. But I remained in the stall."

"Okay, Mom. What did they say?"

"They were discussing Henry and a woman they had seen him with at an earlier time. Sybil was doing the talking, and she said that he fathered a child by that woman. And that Henry received a letter from her informing him of his illegitimate son."

Laura dropped her face in her hands. "Oh, my goodness. Henry started dating another woman after we broke up. I wonder if it was the same person."

Her mother placed her hand on her arm and patted it, but she did not immediately respond to her touch.

Laura took a long swallow of her iced tea and then placed the glass on her napkin.

"Mom, what did you do?"

Her mother straightened her back and said, "I walked out of that stall with my head held high and smiled at my two friends as if I hadn't heard a word. You wouldn't believe the looks on their faces. They were so nervous that I would say something to them."

"I know that look. What did you say?"

"I told them if I ever heard either of them discuss that rumor again, I would sue them for slander." She chuckled. "And, you know, my husband is the district attorney, and he can ruin both of your husbands' banking careers."

Laura put her hand to her mouth and said, "Mom, I can't believe you said that!"

"Well, it wasn't one of my finer moments, but I'm certain it stopped that vicious rumor. However, you must go home and make certain Henry Whelchel never looks at another woman again."

"Now, how am I supposed to make that happen?" Laura cried.

"Well, that's easy. You treat Henry like the king he is in your home. Treat him with kindness and make sure he never looks elsewhere for affection." Her mother reached for her hand, "Do you understand what I mean?"

"Mom, this is the eighties," Laura said. "We don't look at marriage the way women of your generation did."

Her mother pointed her finger at her and said, "Let me tell you something about men. Some are loyal as hell and would never consider running around on their wives. However, others are born with a tendency to be unfaithful, because they are self-centered and think it is their right to be with other women. Or, most often the case, a couple gets busy raising their children and building a life together. As a result, the husband isn't getting the attention he once received at home."

Her mother smiled as she reached for her hand.

"Sweetheart, I know you are busy with a newborn baby, and motherhood takes some adjusting, but you have a responsibility to create a happy family life."

"Well, even if the rumor is true, Henry stayed with me!"

Her mother's eyes were as big as saucers, as she looked toward the kitchen. "Please keep your voice down, honey. You know Minnie listens to our conversations."

"Who cares, Mama? I have nothing to hide."

"I know, my dear. However, you just consider what I told you."

Chapter Eleven

After Laura met with Andrew at the law firm, she stopped by the grocery store before going home. But as she pulled onto Whelchel Road, she noticed an unfamiliar car sitting in the circular drive in front of her house.

Laura parked her car in the garage and went into the kitchen. Fitz sat at the bar, eating a slice of cake while talking to Julia.

"Mom, look who surprised us with a visit this morning."

"I wondered who that shiny Range Rover belonged to," Laura said. "How are you, Fitz?"

Fitz wiped his hands on the napkin, and hugged Laura.

She shot a side glance at Julia and winked.

Julia rolled her eyes and shook her head.

"Can you stay for dinner, Fitz?" Laura asked. "Julia brought food to prepare for dinner tonight, and I picked up a fresh salad while at the market. We would love for you to join us."

She hesitated and then continued with a grin. "I'm sure you didn't come all this way for a slice of homemade cake."

"Well, to be honest, a slice of this cake would be worth the drive over, but I would love to stay for dinner," Fitz said as he smiled at Julia.

"Good, that's settled. Now, I need to change into my farm shoes and take the Gator down to the pasture. I awoke early this morning and remembered that no one had checked on the barn and stable since the weekend Henry went on hospice."

Fitz looked at Julia and asked, "What's a Gator?"

"It's a utility vehicle we use on the farm."

Fitz turned to Laura. "I can go check it out for you."

Laura looked down at his shoes and said, "You can't go down to the barn wearing those expensive shoes."

Julia went out to the garage and found a pair of her dad's work boots and brought them inside. "Here's a pair of boots, try them on. If they fit, I'll ride with you to check on the farm."

While changing shoes, Fitz said, "Why don't you stay up here with your mother while I go down. You have spent no time with her this morning."

Laura agreed with Fitz and asked Julia if she would help her get their lunch ready while Fitz went to the barn. Julia went to the key rack and found the key to the Gator and pitched it over to Fitz as he walked out the back door.

"Do you know how to drive one of those things?" Julia asked.

Fitz laughed as he grabbed the key, "I can operate almost any vehicle, whether it runs on land, air, or sea." Still smiling, he stepped back inside the door and brushed her cheek with a quick kiss.

Later that evening, Fitz entertained them throughout dinner. Laura watched as he interacted with Julia, and she smiled as they enjoyed a friendly banter. Julia was love-struck with Fitz, and how could she not be? His personality was so much like Henry. But Laura could tell they were not intimate.

As he told a story about his childhood, he called his mother by name. "I couldn't have been over six years old, when I turned to Mom in front of the priest and said, Sofia Romano, you did not bake that cake, Grandma did."

Everyone burst into laughter at the punch line of his story. Then Laura recognized his mother's name, the woman Henry dated before they became engaged. Her stomach got queasy when she remembered the letter she found in Henry's desk was just signed SSR.

Sofia Romano. Oh dear, Laura thought, *even her name sounds exotic.*

******

On Sunday morning, while Julia and Betsy went down to the stable to enjoy a quick ride on their horses, Laura and Fitz made brunch. Fitz made a batch of mimosas and poured them each a glass while chopping the fresh veggies, diced the ham, and shredded the cheese to use in the omelets.

While the hash brown potatoes were cooking in the pan, Laura scooped out the fruit and divided it into individual bowls. Then Laura heard a shrilling scream. Startled, Laura looked at Fitz and said, "Did you hear that noise?"

Laura wiped off her hands, cut off the stove, and ran out the kitchen door, while Fitz followed close behind. When they got out on the porch, the girls were waving their hands, both speaking at the same time. Betsy climbed off the Gator and started throwing up. Julia was gulping for air as she tried to talk. "Mom, call the police. We found a decapitated body lodged under a tree limb in the creek near the barn."

Fitz said, "Laura, perhaps I should check it out."

Julia shot Fitz a hard look. "You'd never find the body. It's covered with tree limbs."

"Oh, okay," Fitz replied. "That makes sense."

"Mom, call the police. If you don't, I'll have to use my cellphone. You know they'll stay on the phone until a patrol car arrives on the scene."

Laura patted Fitz's arm.

"Thanks, Fitz," Laura said. "But Julia's right. If we call from the landline, they will see the local number, and it will cause fewer delays."

"Well, I'll stand out front and wait for the patrol car to arrive," Fitz said.

"That's fine." Julia said. "Just send the sheriff to the barn when they get here. I'm going back down to make sure no one disturbs the body. Because of the decomposition of the body, I wonder how long it's been in the creek."

"Seriously, you're going back to the scene of the crime by yourself?" Fitz asked.

Julia laughed at his drama, "Earth to Fitz, remember I'm a nurse practitioner, so the sight of a dead body doesn't bother me. And for the record, the creek behind our farm is not a crime scene. Maybe the body drifted downstream and got lodged between the fallen trees in the water. I'm sure the authorities will not consider the area a crime scene."

Betsy sat down on the stoop, "Fitz, be a gentleman, and get me a Diet Coke from the fridge, please."

"Sure," he said.

Covering her eyes. Betsy said. "I've never seen anything more disgusting in my entire life."

"Fitz grab a cold rag while you're in there. She doesn't look too good." Julia hollered before riding off.

When Fitz went into the kitchen, Laura was talking to the local law enforcement. She turned to Fitz while placing her hand over the receiver. "I'm on hold. Are the girls okay?"

"Betsy's white as a sheet, but Julia's a trouper. It's as if finding a decapitated body on your property is an everyday occurrence."

"Well, people around here lose their lives in the lake, and it often takes some time to recover the bodies. I suspect it will be the case in this situation, too. We'll just have to wait and see."

It was after twelve o'clock when the local authorities began their investigation, looking for evidence about what might have happened. Laura, Betsy, and Fitz were still hanging around the back porch waiting to hear from Julia.

Chapter Twelve

A call came into the local Boone County FBI office at 12:05 p.m. on the day they discovered the body. Bill Bowen, a special agent in charge of the FBI Office in Abington, Georgia, took the call from the field office in Washington, DC.

The DC agent, Roberts, reported that an informant was working inside the Suarez Cartel investigation and missing for over a week. His last known location provided by the informant's cell phone showed a rural area in Boone County, outside the city of Abington. He provided the address of the farm they had under surveillance and instructed Agent Bowen to send a detail out to the area to search for the informant.

"Yes, sir. We're on it. The search will begin at once, sir," Agent Bowen said.

When the call ended, Bowen yelled from his office, "Get in here guys, we just got a call from the big boys in DC. We've got a man missing from an investigation detail."

Agent Bowen searched his desk for the piece of paper, where he had jotted down the address.

"Dammit, where did I put that address? Here it is. Take this address down and follow me. Let's go find out what the hell is going on. And remember, while we are there, keep me posted of anything and everything."

* * * * * * * *

While Julia waited for the authorities to arrive, she found a long stick in the wooded area. She removed as much vegetation from the area surrounding the corpse as possible. Even to her untrained eye, it appeared some clever person placed the body under the tree trunk. The naked torso was exposed, but the bottom part of the body was hidden from view by the tree trunk, leaves, and foliage. Julia suspected the recent rains washed some leaves downstream, which left the upper body visible.

They had stripped the body of its clothing down to its underwear. Because of the frigid winter temperatures, the body appeared to have suffered little decomposition, which suggested the time of death could be earlier than the body seemed to show.

Julia looked up at the sound of sirens and saw two sheriff cars, an ambulance, and a fire truck, followed by a silver SUV.

When the vehicles parked, a sizeable man, with a wad of chewing tobacco stuffed in the cheek of his mouth, got out of the patrol car. "Afternoon, ma'am. I'm Duncan Riley, the Sheriff of Boone County. I hear tell you found a body back here in the creek."

Julia walked over to the sheriff and said, "Yes, sir. Right over there under that enormous pine tree."

The sheriff and his deputies walked to the creek's edge, and Sheriff Riley turned to Julia and said, "Yep! Looks to me like a corpse, all right."

The sheriff chuckled.

"Can't believe you're hanging around down here."

He kicked a limb to the side as he looked around the wooded area.

"You didn't happen to see his head floating around here anywhere, have you?"

"No, sir. I haven't looked for his head, nor have I seen his clothes. I was just staying down here until you guys showed up."

"You say all of his clothes are missing?"

"That's correct."

"That's strange." The sheriff said as he rubbed his chin.

"Yes, it is," Julia said. "If you move to this side of the creek bed, you'll get a better view of the body."

The sheriff looked at his deputies, "You boys get started combing this area near the creek. In the meantime, I'll radio the coroner. He'll get ticked if I don't call him first."

One of the EMT personnel walked over to the patrol car. "Sheriff, do you need more time to investigate before we pull the body from the creek?"

"Heck, yeah." He spat a mouth full of tobacco juice on the ground. "Let's give my boys a few more minutes to comb the area real good. We'll let the coroner tell us when it's time to remove the body."

While Sheriff Riley was on hold with the coroner's office, his deputies reported that they could not find anything suspicious. It appeared no one had been in the wooded area around the creek bed in a while, although they saw some animal tracks.

Julia overheard the conversation.

"Excuse me," Julia said. "Sheriff Riley, my sister and I were riding our horses this morning when we discovered the body in the creek. I suspect those tracks are from our horses."

The sheriff looked at his deputy and said, "Well, that makes sense, those tracks look fresh to me."

Three black, unmarked SUV's with tinted windows sped down the one-lane road toward the barn, followed by a cloud of dust. As soon as they reached the barn area, the drivers slammed on the brakes as their vehicles slid sideways, and two men then jumped out of each vehicle, flashing their badges in unison.

Sheriff Riley widened his stance and folded his arms high at his chest, his eyes never leaving the vehicles.

"Now, who in the hell called the FBI?" The sheriff shook his head.

Julia shrugged. "Who knows."

"Dag-gum-it, it's apparent the boy drowned and then floated along in the water. Bet a recreational boat severed the body. We shore don't need the FBI down here".

"Agent Bill Bowen, FBI." He continued to hold his badge out in front of him. "Who's in charge here?"

In a strong southern drawl, the sheriff said. "That would be me." His tobacco juice landed on the ground, almost hitting Agent Bowen's shoes.

Looking up, Bowen said, "The FBI is in charge now. You are free to leave. We will take over from here."

"Listen here, mister," said the sheriff. "This is my jurisdiction, and my men will leave when I get good and damn ready for them to leave."

The remaining FBI agents combed the area while Agent Bowen talked with the sheriff.

An agent approached Bowen. "Sir, can you step over here a minute? This appears to be a homicide."

"Yes. I'll be there in a second."

While walking toward the agent, Bowen looked back over his shoulder. "Sheriff, you're done here."

Chapter Thirteen

L aura scrolled through her phone while standing at the bar in the kitchen, waiting for the coffee to finish brewing. It was already March 16, 2014, when she realized one month had passed since Henry's funeral.

Henry's financial advisor, Rhett Louis, called and scheduled a meeting with her regarding Henry's portfolio. For reasons unclear to Laura, Henry never introduced her to his financial advisor.

Mr. Louis was a known womanizer, and because she was timid around strangers, Laura prepared for a short but productive meeting.

The time was later than she thought. She reached for her favorite mug, filled it with coffee, and headed toward the shower. Laura had an appointment with Jane at J. Green Salon, to get her hair styled before the meeting.

Before going to bed the previous night, she chose a conservative outfit to wear to the appointment. Still, she was careful not to select anything that would make her look too matronly.

An hour and a half later, as she entered the front door of the office building where Mr. Louis worked, she paused to appreciate the beautiful works of art hanging throughout the foyer. Captivated by the brilliant fall colors of an oil painting signed by a local artist, Laura studied the aerial view of the landscape of the hills and valleys drawn during the autumn season.

Laura felt as if she were being watched, and she turned and saw an attractive man leaning against the door with a sexy smile on his face.

The man asked. "May I help you, young lady?"

Embarrassed that his reference to a young lady would please her, she rolled her eyes and said, "No, thanks. I have an appointment to meet with Mr. Louis."

Rhett smiled as he walked toward her and extended a hand. "I'm Rhett Louis. I assume you are Mrs. Whelchel."

Laura moistened her lips. She could feel her flushed face as she responded, "Yes, I'm Laura Whelchel. It's nice to meet you, Mr. Louis."

"Please Laura, call me Rhett."

As he directed her onto the elevator, he said, "I was expecting someone much older."

Laura turned her head to mask the smile on her face.

On the third level of the building, his penthouse office was well-appointed with sleek, modern furniture. However, the expensive furnishings paled compared to the city's panoramic view, visible from the ceiling to floor windows, which occupied an entire office wall.

Someone had prepared an elaborate PowerPoint presentation of the diverse portfolio held by Henry Whelchel. Rhett was knowledgeable in his explanation of the percentages, the recent Return on Investments, and the projections of profits for five years. Laura watched Rhett with interest as he moved around the office, explaining the necessity for a balanced portfolio.

Laura felt her burning cheeks. For over thirty-five years, people knew her as Henry's wife, and now being a widow for less than two months, the feelings she experienced sitting across from this attractive man seemed unnatural.

When Rhett finished the presentation, he sat in the club chair next to her and crossed his long, slender legs.

"Now, Laura, as you can tell, Henry has left you in an excellent financial position. Provided there are no outstanding debts, the income from these investments will carry you through a long and prosperous life. If you don't mind a suggestion, perhaps you will consider adding to these investments with part of the proceeds from Henry's life insurance policy." He paused and waited for a response.

Laura hesitated to speak.

Instead, she stood up.

Then he stood, too.

She went to the window to create space between them, but he followed and stood next to her. When she looked at him, he was only a few inches away, so close that she detected the hint of a breath mint.

With a charming smile, he leaned a little closer and placed his hand on top of hers, "Are you all right, Laura?"

His lingering touch startled her. But there was something in the way he spoke her name that caused her to blush.

"Oh, yes. I'm fine. I just wanted to look at this beautiful view. Henry once told me the view at night was spectacular. Now that I'm here, I can easily see that he was correct."

"Perhaps you can come back late one afternoon before dusk," he said, "and experience the view for yourself."

"That would be lovely."

Within fifteen minutes of arriving, she gathered her pocketbook and was back in the elevator. As she walked through the lobby, she glanced at the painting and wondered if it was painted from an aerial picture of her farm."

Chapter Fourteen

A t the two-month mark, just as promised, Andrew Byrd contacted Laura to schedule a meeting. Initially, he suggested including the girls, but Laura didn't have the stamina to deal with another public outburst by her youngest daughter. Betsy had given her nothing but problems since Henry's passing.

The meeting began by reviewing their assets. Andrew tried to hide his disappointment as he explained the gravity of her debt load. "Before we get into specifics about Henry's debt, I wanted to remind you that the doctor released Theo Williams to return to work. It seems he has recovered from the heart attack. May I suggest we meet with Theo as soon as possible to discuss any profits you are due from the industrial park investment?"

"Excuse me, Andrew," Laura said. "I'm not following you. We never invested in Theo's industrial park project."

"Yes, Henry was one of the first to invest. Therefore, there should be some profits coming to you soon."

Laura's hand shook as she picked up the envelope in her lap. Then she took a deep breath. "One would think to invest in a project of that magnitude, even in a partnership capacity, would require a sizable amount of cash. Do you agree?"

"Listen, Theo and Claire are coming over for dinner tonight, and Daisy wanted me to ask you to join us. Perhaps we can corner Theo tonight, and ask him about it before dinner, without making a big deal about the situation."

"Andrew, I need some answers. It seems like every few days since Henry's death, I've had another problem dropped in my lap. So, please, let's be honest with each other. I have yet to find the insurance policy that Henry discussed canceling because of the increased premiums at his sixty-fifth birthday. One policy I found was for the partner liability. The other one covered a debt at the bank, of which I was totally unaware. There's an outstanding mortgage on my home, on which I am now struggling to make payments. Unless we find another policy or have a windfall profit from Theo's industrial project, then I'm ruined." Her bottom lip quivered as she paused and reached for a Kleenex and dabbed at her eyes.

Andrew removed his glasses and rubbed his temples.

"You know, a day or so after Henry died," Laura said, "I had a premonition that I would be forced to sell the farm to keep the house. But I realize now my home must go, too."

"Let's not count it lost, not just yet. Come over to the house tonight for dinner, and I'll find a way to get an answer from Theo, so you'll know whether you must sell both the farm and the house."

"Then, do you agree," Laura said, "that I'm facing a forced sale of my property?"

"If we don't find another policy or additional assets, then yes, I agree.

Chapter Fifteen

A
s Laura freshened up before going over to Andrew and
Daisy's for dinner, Claire called to suggest they pick her up
on their way over. Laura put on the last touches of makeup
and then turned out the overhead light in her bathroom before going
into the kitchen to wait for her ride.

The phone rang as she walked into the kitchen. As she answered,
Laura expected to hear the voice of one of her girls. She put the phone
on speaker.

"Hello, ma'am. This is Special Agent, Bill Bowen, from the field
office of the Federal Bureau of Investigation. With whom am I
speaking?"

"The FBI. What do you want with me?"

"Ma'am, may I have your name, please?"

"If you are with the FBI, shouldn't you know my name?"

"Yes, ma'am. I have your name. However, I'm trying to confirm
you as the person who owns property on Whelchel Road in southern
Abington. Would that be you?"

"Yes. I own property on Whelchel Road. We named the road after
my late husband, Henry Whelchel. We are the only farm on this road."

"And Mrs. Whelchel, your first name is...."

"I apologize, Special Agent Bowen, is that correct?"

"Yes, ma'am."

"My name is Laura Whelchel."

"Thank you, Mrs. Whelchel. I am in the area, and I'd like to drop by your house. We need to review the information about the body found on your property last month. It will only take a few minutes of your time."

Laura hesitated.

"If it doesn't take too long. I'm going over to a friend's house for dinner in about an hour."

"Yes. I promise it'll only take ten to fifteen minutes."

It wasn't long before she heard a car coming down the road.

Laura watched as the black, unmarked SUV pulled into the circular drive. She met the agent at the door and invited him into the kitchen. They sat at the bar as Agent Bowen explained the ongoing investigation involving their agent who disappeared.

Agent Bowen asked her questions about any unusual individuals hanging around her property.

"Was there anyone, let's say, whose presence might have seemed out of place during that period?"

"Do you suspect the death of your agent was a homicide? And why would you suspect anyone to be hanging around *my* farm? I'm sorry if I'm asking too many questions. However, my concern about what has happened is genuine."

"No, Mrs. Whelchel, I expected you to have questions. But I'm just trying to find out if anyone other than your regular family members and friends were on your property?"

Laura put her head back and looked at the ceiling and said, "No. But the week following Henry's death, many people were dropping off food and such, but they were all people we've known for years. There was no one suspicious hanging around, I guess I'm trying to say."

"Okay, I appreciate your honesty. I realize this has been a tough time for you. It is unusual for a property owner to find a dead body on their land."

"Well, one thing that I've noticed lately is the increase in helicopter traffic, especially during the early morning hours and late afternoon."

"The FBI sometimes watches large, wooded areas searching for illegal drug crops. More recently, we have been looking for areas that would make for convenient drug drops." The agent said, "So, you may continue to notice the afternoon chopper surveys."

"Well, how do you explain the presence of the morning choppers?"

"I apologize, but I haven't been privy to that information."

Agent Bowen turned on his laptop and said, "I've been directed to get the names of everyone staying here during the week the body was discovered."

Laura looked at him with furrowed brows.

"This is just protocol for any death within the bureau."

"My daughter, Julia, provided that information to you on the day of the search."

"We have reason to believe there was someone else staying at your house during that weekend…maybe your daughter failed to mention," he said. "Believe me, it is perfectly normal for someone to omit a name, especially when there's so much going on… We're just trying to tie up the loose ends of this investigation."

"I can email a file with the names of everyone who came to my home that weekend, and the nature of their visit. Will that work?"

Bowen opened the document and noted Laura's spreadsheet made it easier to identify the names of everyone who visited the Whelchel farm during that weekend. He confirmed the names listed on his report, except for one person.

"Thank you so much, Mrs. Whelchel," he said. "It appears the names match the list provided by your daughter, with one exception, a Mr. Fitzgerald Romano."

Chapter Sixteen

Laura stood in the kitchen door as she watched for Claire and Theo to arrive. When she saw their car lights in the drive, she grabbed her pocketbook and went out the door. It was a quick drive to the Byrd's home, which passed with only a brief comment from Claire, who talked about the weather.

Laura remained silent as she sat in the backseat. She couldn't understand why Julia hadn't disclosed Fitz's name to the FBI agent when questioned.

When she walked inside her friend's house, she tried to forget about the visit from Agent Bowen. Still, it stayed in the back of her mind throughout the evening.

****

While the ladies were in the kitchen, Andrew poured a drink for his guest.

He looked toward the women in the other room, Andrew lowered his voice and said, "I need to ask you a question."

"Of course, Andrew. What is it?"

"Does Henry have any profits due to him, from his investment in the industrial park? You know, I would never ask you anything about your business, but our friend's wife is experiencing temporary financial pressure. You know how these things go, until we gain access to all of Henry's financial statements and insurance policies, her cash flow is going to be tight."

"I understand. Let me look at it tomorrow, and I'll get back with you."

"Thanks, my friend. We need to take care of our own. Henry would do the same for us."

As they sat down to dinner, Andrew watched Laura as she played with her food.

"Theo, how does it feel to get back to work, my friend?" Andrew asked.

Theo smiled as he looked around the table. "It feels great to have someplace to go each day. I never realized how much I would miss my work. And, I must admit, Teddy has done an impressive job running the business in my absence."

There was a silence in the room as Daisy asked, "Laura, have you heard any more about the body that was found on your property?"

Claire raised her eyebrows as she looked at Daisy.

"Well, I had a visit this afternoon from Agent Bowen, with the FBI's local field office. It appears they are tying up the loose ends of the investigation involving the body found behind my property."

"Have they identified the body yet?" Daisy asked.

"They're close. He confirmed they would use the fingerprints as identification. So, I'm hoping that is one more thing to mark off my list."

"Did they ever determine how the agent was killed?" Claire asked.

"Agent Bowen did not disclose any details about how he died. He questioned me about any unusual activity that might've taken place on my property. He wanted to confirm the people staying at the house the weekend the body was discovered. It was just a friendly visit to confirm the information we'd already provided."

"It's hard to imagine the FBI paying a friendly social visit to anyone," Daisy said. "Perhaps, I watch too much television."

Daisy laughed.

"Laura," Claire said. "We must forgive our friend, Daisy, between the television shows and those murder mysteries she reads, I'm surprised Andrew doesn't sleep with a gun under the bed."

Andrew shook his head as he laughed. "Don't think I haven't considered it."

"Laura, how are the girls holding up?" Daisy asked. "We have seen little of them around town since the funeral."

"Of course, Marsha is back at work at the college. She seems to be working through her grief with no problem. And Julia has a new love interest. You guys met him at the funeral."

Laura paused and covered her mouth with her napkin.

"And then there's Betsy, Henry's sweet little Betsy," Laura said with a nervous laugh as tears escaped her eyes. "She's the one that continues to cause me to worry... I'm sure it'll all work out."

Laura folded her napkin and said, "Daisy, thank you for this delicious meal. You know how much I love grilled salmon."

****

After dinner, the ladies followed Daisy into the kitchen. They were cleaning up a bit while refilling their wine glasses.

"Laura, what can Daisy and I do to help?" Claire asked. "You must have a million things that need handling, and we would love to be of help."

"Thank you, both." Smiling, Laura moved her wrist to her heart, then gestured to her friends.

"I'm just trying to keep my head above water. Henry was a wonderful husband, father, and provider. However, we made a few decisions before his death, which has altered my lifestyle. That period was such a difficult time for us, and we didn't give some of those decisions enough consideration. I realize, now, that it'll take a while to work through it all."

"Well, what can we do to help?" Daisy asked.

"Nothing that comes to mind. But that's a sweet offer. I've got to make some hard decisions very soon about my living arrangements. I'm living on a tight budget for the first time in my adult life."

Theo stuck his head in the kitchen and asked Claire and Laura if they were prepared to leave. He told them that since his heart attack occurred, he was sleepy by nine o'clock each night, and he was ready to go home and get into bed. Andrew laughed and reminded them of how Henry would fall asleep and miss the card game they used to play when they got together.

Laura said, "That explains the reason we were usually the last to leave. Henry was sleeping!"

Chapter Seventeen

On the way home, Theo mentioned to Laura that Henry had partnered with him in the industrial park project and that he would like to sit down with her to discuss the investment at a convenient time.

When Laura got out of the car, Claire and Theo watched as she waved from the front porch.

"Theo, Laura's going through a hard time right now. Is there any way we can offer her some financial assistance without her feeling that it is a handout?"

"That really isn't our concern. I'm sure it's just a matter of time before everything will get sorted out, and she will be fine."

"No, I don't believe that will happen," Claire said. "Laura is living on a tight budget, trying to make a mortgage payment that she knew nothing about."

"Well, give me some time. I'll look at the partnership agreement and review the finances. I'm hopeful that we'll find some money for Laura. Henry discussed buying a partnership policy, but I'm not sure if he followed through on it. Anyway, that'll be the first thing I do when I get to the office tomorrow. Please don't worry about this, honey. It'll work out."

"Theo, we live a life of privilege, and we have more money than we could spend in two lifetimes. We need to help Laura, even if it means giving her our profits from the project. Developing the industrial park was never about the money. It was about fulfilling a dream. And, thankfully, you're still here pursuing that dream. And our friend, Henry, isn't."

He reached over and patted Claire's hand. "You're a good woman, Claire Williams."

Later, when they went to bed, Theo found it impossible to sleep. He tossed and turned as he thought about Henry's financial situation. But how was he to know that Henry leveraged everything to take part in the project? It surprised him to learn that Henry took out a new mortgage on their home that he paid off years earlier. That didn't sound like a man with a finance background.

Theo got up before the alarm went off, showered and was at the office by 7:00 a.m.

He had already reviewed the partnership agreement when his assistant arrived. But as he suspected, Henry had failed to follow through and purchase the partnership policy. Then he remembered when they drew up the partnership agreement, Henry was diagnosed with cancer. So, it would have been futile to apply for an insurance policy anyway, because of his health issues.

Looking at the surplus in their checking account, he decided to give Laura two thousand dollars each month until Andrew could settle Henry's estate. As he thought about his friend's predicament, he coughed to suppress the lump in his throat.

Henry, I sure miss you, buddy.

Theo removed his handkerchief from his jacket. Then he rolled his chair over to the picture window and watched the sunrise into the clear sky. He was so moved by the glorious display of colors, that he lifted his face to the heavens and thanked God that he'd survived his heart attack.

Chapter Eighteen

L aura went straight home after she met again with Andrew. She walked through the house and made mental notes of the furnishings she wanted to keep. There were several expensive items she could sell to help pay down the mortgage at the bank. Andrew had suggested selling the farm first, which would allow her to stay in the house a while longer.

She finished making a pot of coffee when the doorbell rang in the foyer. Laura walked through the dining room, peeked out the window, and saw Theo standing in the circular drive with his cell phone to his ear. She opened the door and motioned for him to come into the house.

"Hello, Laura. How are you today?" Theo said.

"I'm doing okay."

They walked into the kitchen.

"Would you like a cup of coffee and a slice of Daisy's pound cake?"

"Sure," Theo said. "But promise not to tell Claire."

They both laughed.

While sitting at the bar, Laura asked how long it would take to sell the farm, and how much she could expect to clear from the sale. Theo was cautious in delivering the information.

"You won't believe this, Laura, but I have three inquiries already for your property this morning."

"What do you mean?"

"We posted your property on our website yesterday afternoon. There are pictures, land dimensions, and a caption that the property will soon be available for sale."

"Isn't that somewhat premature, since I haven't signed the contract yet?"

"Perhaps," Theo said. "However, one of the interested parties sent over an offer this morning, and although I plan to counter, it gives us a starting point,"

He reached over the chair, opened the briefcase, and placed a manila folder on the bar. He had clipped a check to the folder. Theo handed it to Laura and explained that the two-thousand-dollars represented some profits generated by Henry's investment in the industrial park project.

When Laura looked down at the check, tears formed in her eyes. The mortgage payment was due in two days, and until now, she didn't know how she would make that payment, besides paying her other expenses.

She fought back tears. "Thank you, Theo," Laura said. "This is such an unexpected blessing."

"Well, if you find that amount a blessing, wait until you see the number on this contract."

Theo slid the paper across the bar so Laura could see the offer listed on the front page. She looked at the document, and then looked up at Theo and asked, "Is this a legitimate offer?"

"It is indeed."

The offer for six hundred thousand dollars was much more than Andrew had suggested she get for the farm. With that kind of money, she could pay off the medical bills and most of the mortgage, which would allow her to stay in her home for a while longer.

Chapter Nineteen

T hree weeks after the offer for the property was accepted, Laura stood outside the barn. She watched the team from Lake Estate Sales as they inventoried the farm equipment and machinery and assigned a price to each item.

She expected Theo to drop by the farm.

His shiny, black Mercedes crept down the dirt road to the barn, a few moments later.

When Theo got out of the car, he hesitated a few moments before he walked over to where Laura stood. "We've re-negotiated the original offer for the land minus two acres for the house. I'm here to ask the man in charge of the sale to consider selling the equipment in bulk. Are you in agreement?"

After a few moments of negotiations, the owner of the company agreed.

When the team completed assigning value to each item, the number was more than Theo had expected. Theo called the buyer's realtor and proposed the amount assessed for the farm equipment.

"Well, that was easy," Theo said. "After consulting with the buyer, they've agreed to pay the additional two hundred and fifty thousand dollars for the equipment."

"Thank you, Theo, the proceeds from the property, including the equipment, will allow me to pay off the debts and have enough money to buy a small place in the city."

Theo touched her arm. "That's wonderful news, Laura. I'm glad this worked out."

After finalizing the property and equipment negotiations, Laura drove the Gator back up to the garage. When she went inside the house, the emotional attachment was no longer there. In her heart, she had already moved.

Once she realized selling the property was necessary, and with the farm equipment already included in the deal, Laura was ready to move on to the next chapter in her life.

The phone rang, which jolted her back to reality.

"Hello Julia. How are you, dear?"

After a few moments of small talk, the conversation turned to Fitz. Laura asked if Julia had met Mrs. Romano. Julia explained that she had interviewed the in-home staff Fitz hired to provide care for his mom.

"Well, I would like to invite Fitz and his mother for a visit. I'm hopeful Marsha and Betsy can come, too. This farm will be sold soon, and I would like you all to come home for one last visit over the weekend. Besides, it would be a perfect time for me to meet Fitz's mom. What do you think about that idea, Julia?"

"Okay, Mom. But, please keep in mind, Mrs. Romano is terminal."

"I know she is, honey, but she may enjoy a trip to the country. Perhaps a change of scenery will do her good."

****

Laura was in the kitchen cutting fruit for lunch, when she heard a noise from the backyard. She looked outside the window and saw Julia holding the car door open while Fitz picked up his mother and placed her in the wheelchair. Laura wiped her hands and waited for them to get inside before she greeted them.

"Hello, my dear. I'm Laura Whelchel, and it's nice to finally meet you."

Mrs. Romano remained silent.

Fitz, then noticed the startled look upon his mother's face, as he said, "Laura, this is my mother, Mia Romano. Mom, this is Laura."

Laura extended her hand, "It's so nice to meet you, Mia. Welcome to my home."

Stunned at meeting Laura for the first time, Mia's voice grew timid, "Thank you."

While everyone got settled in, Laura continued to work on the lunch. Mia rolled her wheelchair back into the kitchen and said, "Your home is lovely, Laura."

"Thank you."

"I didn't realize your last name was Whelchel, until Fitz introduced us a few moments ago. When I first moved to Georgia, and that's been over thirty years ago, I knew of a family named Whelchel."

"Tell me, Mia, how did you end up here?"

****

Mia shared that her family had sent her to America because the family's prominent position in the region would be threatened once they learned of her marriage to an Italian.

"Goodness," Laura said. "That must have been a scary experience. What happened?"

"My family was very strict, and they felt I had violated their trust by marrying a foreigner," Mia said. "To conceal my indiscretion, my father arranged for the purchase of a one-way plane ticket to the States."

Mia described the fear of landing at the Atlanta airport, without knowing anyone. The first couple of days, she hung out in the airport, and fortunately for her, she met a nice woman in the coffee shop. The woman from Macon, Georgia, happened to be a member of the business office at Mercer University. She told Mia of a law school position that required a bilingual person, fluent in Spanish, because of the student body's increased diversity. Mia rode the bus to Macon and spent the night in a motel near the university. The next day, she interviewed for the position, and was hired immediately because she was the only fluent Spanish-speaking applicant.

Laura asked, "So when you arrived, you had no place to stay?"

"That's correct, and I didn't know a single person here."

Mia explained that the interviewer noticed the suitcase which rested next to her chair, and realized that she probably needed a place to live. He then offered to rent her an apartment over his garage, which was located less than one mile from the law school office. Mia laughed as she remembered the weekly rent of twenty-five dollars, and explained that she accepted his offer for the apartment, sight unseen.

When Julia walked into the kitchen to get a bottle of water out of the fridge, Mia slowly spoke softer and softer at the end of the story about her arrival into the United States. As Mia continued to watch Julia move around the kitchen, it occurred to her that Fitz was possibly seeing his half-sister. Until now, Mia hadn't realized Julia's maiden name was Whelchel. If she knew, she would have discouraged Fitz from becoming involved with her. Quietly, she watched as Julia interacted with her mother. They were more like sisters than mother and daughter. Julia was the spitting image of Laura, with her blonde hair and petite frame. The only resemblance to Henry was the softness of her brown eyes.

A loud commotion was heard from the back door. When she turned to see who was making the noise, Mia's eyes grew large as she saw a female version of Henry Whelchel entering the kitchen. Marsha was taller than Julia, and her skin coloring was a deep olive that paired well against her dark brown hair. The closer Marsha moved in her direction. The weaker Mia became. Feeling dizzy, Mia experienced a sudden sense of falling, and then her world turned completely black.

****

When Mia awoke, she was strapped to a gurney in the back of an ambulance heading to the local hospital. Everything was blurred, and although she understood the conversation between the EMT personnel and Julia, she lost consciousness again.

Mia was busy filing away her daily reports when she looked up and saw Henry coming toward the building. He must be finished with class early today, she thought. When Henry walked through the door, he stopped and smiled at her, but said nothing.

"What is it, Henry? What are you smiling about?" Mia asked.

"I just found out that classes have been canceled for Thursday and Friday, and I thought we might head to the coast for a long weekend."

"Henry, I can't just run off to the beach like that. I have a job!"

"Well, you get vacation days, don't you?"

The next time Mia awakened, she was in the ICU, while Laura sat next to her bed.

A smile formed on Mia's face, and when Laura noticed she was awake, she tried to console her. "I'm fine, really, Laura. What happened?"

"My oldest daughter had just gotten home for the weekend, and I believe all of the excitement caused you to faint and fall from your chair. The doctors think you may have a concussion. They have been running a battery of tests to determine the seriousness of your condition. They're concerned about why you have been drifting in and out of consciousness, since you arrived at the hospital yesterday afternoon."

Mia reached for Laura's hand, and with labored breath, "We need to talk... there is something you must know."

"Of course, Mia, what is it?"

Mia took a deep breath, and her eyes became heavy again as Laura tried to talk to her. But, despite her best efforts, Mia lost consciousness again...

Henry picked Mia up from her office around noon on Thursday, and they headed to St. Simons Island. There wasn't a cloud in sight, and Henry had suggested riding with the windows rolled down. Of course, Mia didn't object, because she had missed the tropical climate of her native country, and the warm sunshine felt good. She packed them a lunch of pimento and cheese sandwiches, potato salad, and they picked up a bucket of chicken on the way out of town. Before they reached the interstate, Henry was already begging her for a piece of chicken and a sandwich.

The trip was the first time they traveled together, and she secretly pretended they were married. When they checked in at the King and Prince Resort, Mia suddenly became nervous with excitement and was anxious to get to their room.

As soon as they walked into the beautifully appointed luxury suite, the anxiety melted away. There was a huge king-size bed, with a loveseat and chair along with other traditionally styled furnishings.

Mia was surprised to find a small refrigerator unit and a coffee machine complete with condiments sitting on the bar. The French doors led out to a covered porch where she found a small, round table with two chairs overlooking the beach. This was a perfect place for a romantic dinner!

"Henry, when we get back up from the beach, we can eat our dinner out here on the porch," Mia said as she clapped with excitement.

Henry, however, had other plans. "Let's go ahead and eat our dinner before going down to the beach."

"Okay, if you'll open the bottle of wine, I'll get everything set up on the porch."

He looked around for the wine and discovered that Mia had packed two wine glasses for their trip.

"You certainly do spoil me, girl," Henry said. "You have really put a lot of thought into the planning of our trip."

Mia giggled as she finished setting the table.

"Well, I couldn't expect you to drink wine from a paper cup."

After they finished eating, they changed clothes and headed to the beach. As the sunset and darkness enveloped them, Henry spread out his towel close to the rock barriers and encouraged Mia to do the same. The reflection of the moonlight sparkled as the waves rolled toward them. The only other light was from a shrimp boat that could be seen on the distant horizon.

However, Mia watched the silhouette of Henry's firm body as he finished the last of his wine. Then, he removed his shirt and gently wrapped his glass inside for protection.

Henry turned to Mia and began to passionately kiss her lips. Immediately, she felt his desire, which surprised her. There was something in the salt air that caused Henry to forget his inhibitions. Their bodies molded into one as they moved with the motion of the crashing waves as the tide swept onto the beach.

Laura stepped out of the unit while one of the nurses got her a Diet Coke. An hour later, when she went back in, Mia was awake.

"Where is Fitz?" Mia asked.

"The nurses insisted that Fitz, and the girls get some rest. I agreed to stay with you until they returned. They'll be back in a few hours to visit."

"What time is it now?"

"It's not quite two o'clock," Laura answered.

"Laura, there is something that I must tell you."

"Of course. What is it?"

Mia spent the next few minutes explaining about the relationship she had while working at Mercer University. She told Laura how she had met a law student who came into her office to get a class changed. He asked her to join him for coffee that evening, and they ended up having a short, three-month affair.

One night he told her that he would be graduating at the end of the semester and planned to return to his hometown to marry his high school sweetheart. Although they had been broken up since the beginning of the year, he now wanted her back. Henry explained while a life with her would be full of excitement, laughter, and romance, his girl back home had family connections necessary in growing a successful law practice.

"Mia, that must have been very hurtful for you to accept."

"Well, yes. He was the first man that I ever truly loved, and I was in this country all alone." She paused for a few moments and gathered her thoughts, and then continued her story. "At the time he broke up with me, I didn't know that I was pregnant. But when the baby was a year old, I wrote him a letter and sent him a picture of our baby."

There were tears in Laura's eyes as she envisioned a young Mia, alone in a foreign country without family, trying to reach out to the father of her young child.

"Did you ever hear any more from him?"

"No. I never did, but I understand why. My friend had a loving wife and a beautiful family. He was a man of conviction who chose to stand by his decision."

Before she could finish telling Laura the complete story, Mia slipped into another state of unconsciousness...

Henry came back into the suite just as Mia was waking. He had been to the beach for a quick run and had found driftwood that had washed up from the surf.

"What do you have there, sweetie?" she asked.

"I picked us up a couple of muffins for breakfast." He placed them on the counter and turned back to Mia.

"And this, is a piece of wood that swept onto the beach overnight. I'm going to make something for you to remember this trip."

He went out to the porch, removed his pocketknife, and carved a heart with their initials into the wood.

She tried to wake up from her dream state, but she kept drifting back to her sweet memories of Henry...

When Mia returned from a doctor's appointment, where she learned about her pregnancy, she sat at her desk and stared at the driftwood. She reached inside her desk drawer and removed a piece of white paper and a pen. Although Mia intended to write Henry a letter explaining her current situation, after an hour of staring at the driftwood, Mia picked up the paper and shredded it into tiny pieces. She thought, how can I ruin Henry's life with news of my pregnancy. He has made his decision, and now I must figure out a way to live with myself.

Ironically, the driftwood was the only gift he had ever given to her other than the baby she now carried inside her body. The loneliness she experienced was unbearable, and unlike anything she had ever known. Tears streamed down her face as she placed the pen back inside the desk drawer. Mia reached for her pocketbook and left the office and walked the short distance to her apartment.

Chapter Twenty

Julia said, "Mom, Betsy called, and they'll be here in time for dinner. Since you've been at the hospital all day, have you given any thought to what we're gonna cook tonight?"

Laura planned to make eggplant parmesan because it was Betsy's favorite meal. She removed the marinara sauce from the freezer to defrost on the counter while preparing the eggplant. Laura prayed while making dinner that Betsy's visit would be uneventful. It seemed that every time she came home, her mood was darker and more volatile than the previous visit.

When Betsy got there, she was alone. Laura could only imagine why Hal and the boys stayed home.

When Laura finished preparing dinner and was plating their food, Julia opened a bottle of wine. She saw the faraway look on Betsy's face that meant her mind was a thousand miles away. Betsy was a dreamer. As a child, she always lived in a world of make-believe.

"Honey, are you staying the night, or will you be driving back after dinner?" Betsy didn't answer. And Laura didn't pursue the conversation.

During dinner, Laura mentioned that the contract on the farm had been signed by both parties. She explained to the girls that the buyer had also offered to purchase the machinery and equipment, which had given them an additional sum of money to help pay off the debt.

"I've been thinking about whether to keep this house."

Betsy threw her head back and looked at the ceiling as she dropped her fork on the table. "Well, where are you going to live, Mom? Have you given that any thought?"

Julia shot a sideways glance at her sister and said, "Betsy. Please calm down. She's just opening a line of discussion here."

"Okay, fine," Betsy persisted. "But have you given any thought about where you might go if you sell our home?"

"Well, honey. I don't know. But, since your father died, this house is just too big for one person. There's a lot involved in maintaining a home of this size."

Betsy smirked. And then she shook her head.

"This is where we grew up," Betsy said. "And Dad would want you to keep this house in the family."

Laura continued to pick at her food as she considered her daughter's hurtful tone. She knew Betsy was heartbroken. Still, they were all hurting, and inflicting pain on each other would only divide her family.

"Honey, it's not a decision we need to make immediately. But I wanted you girls to know that I'm exploring my options."

"Mom, have you discussed selling the house to Marsha?" Julia asked.

Laura shook her head. "No, honey. I was at the hospital with Mia when she left to go back home, and I didn't get a chance to mention it."

Betsy pounded her fist on the table. "Well, we're going to call her as soon as we finish dinner. Marsha needs to know you're thinking about selling our home. She won't like it one bit."

While Laura was cleaning the dishes, she told Julia that she needed to clear out Henry's law office. She explained that Andrew had been patient and had not pushed her to remove his personal items. Julia agreed to go with her the next morning.

Betsy brought the linen napkins from the dining room into the kitchen and said, "Let's go into Dad's study and call Marsha. I'm interested in what she has to say about selling the house."

When they got Marsha on the phone and explained the situation, Marsha immediately agreed that selling the house was a wise decision. She had already checked on several condominiums and cottage-style homes in the surrounding area. Marsha's comments encouraged Laura, and when Julia learned of her sister's research, she suggested they take a weekend off and check it out.

Betsy grabbed her cell phone and went up to bed as soon as the call with Marsha ended.

Laura and Julia stayed in the study for a while longer, and Laura struggled with how best to bring up the subject of Fitz. As much as she felt that Julia's relationship with Fitz should end, she still wasn't sure that Fitz was Henry's illegitimate son. However, things sure pointed in that direction.

Chapter Twenty-One

L aura and Julia got up early. Julia was working the eleven to seven shifts that evening, and she'd planned to return to her apartment for a few hours of sleep before going to work.

They pulled into the law office's parking lot around nine-thirty, which was around the time Henry typically went to work each day.

For some reason, walking into her husband's office was much more emotional than Laura anticipated.

"This is where your father labored to provide a living for us, Julia. There were days he worked fourteen to sixteen hours, especially during those early years, when he was trying criminal cases."

"I know, Mom," Julia said as she hugged her mother. "But Dad loved practicing law."

"He did, indeed."

Laura and Julia walked around and looked at the many awards, framed degrees, and pictures that men of his age group typically displayed in their offices. There were many subtle reminders that he was a family man. Henry maintained memberships with several

111

professional organizations. But he was civic-minded, too. He was a member of the Chamber of Commerce, The Rotary Club, and the local country club.

As she looked at each item on the bookshelf, she picked up the professional picture taken during their last family vacation at St. Simons Island. The guys wore white polo shirts and navy-blue shorts, and the girls wore white blouses and white shorts or Capri pants. They had posed with their backs to the ocean as they stood on the grassy area behind The King and Prince Resort. Laura smiled at the memory.

I've never even sat at this desk before. In fact, I can count on my hands the few occasions that I've been in this room.

Then Laura turned and lovingly placed her hand on the high-backed, leather chair.

She'd never experienced the perspective from her husband's side of the office. But as she sat behind the desk, she noticed the elevated chair and the desk sat on pieces of wood that raised it a good four inches from the ground.

I wonder if Henry used the raised desk to intimidate his clients, so he could get to the truth faster.

As Julia wrapped the pictures in the newspaper and packed them in Tupperware totes, Laura opened each drawer of Henry's desk. There were the usual items found in the middle desk drawer. It had a plastic tray with dividers that separated the rubber bands from paperclips and other miscellaneous items. There was a section for black pens and another for blue. The organization of the drawer was meticulous, characteristic of one Henry would maintain.

The second drawer she opened contained a stack of legal pads, each filled with notes regarding a specific case. There were markings on the side margins and checkmarks over the paragraphs notating the work was completed.

She opened another drawer that stored a tin of cashew nuts and a plastic container filled with peppermint candy. Stashed in the far end of the drawer was a bottle of Double Oaked Woodford Reserve, several whiskey glasses, and an opened pack of white cocktail napkins.

Julia had almost finished packing up the personal items when Laura opened the last drawer of her husband's desk. There were several manilla envelopes positioned horizontally, which Laura removed and placed on top of the desk.

As she was about to close the drawer, she noticed a small white envelope stuck in the back.

She reached for the envelope, and when she opened it, she found a picture of a lovely young woman, walking along a beach, wearing a swimsuit with a colorful sarong around her waist. The woman's complexion was a medium olive color, offset by shiny dark hair, and big, black eyes. She was exotic and beautiful, and unlike anyone Laura had ever seen.

Before Julia saw it, Laura placed the picture back into the envelope and shoved it deep inside her pocketbook.

One by one, she went through the manilla envelopes and made stacks of the documents.

The third one from the top had the initials SSR on the outside. Laura's heart skipped a beat.

Good lord, here's another envelope with her initials written on the front.

Inside, she found a one-million-dollar life insurance policy issued by Mutual of Omaha. The beneficiary was Sofia Suarez Romano, and The Estate of Henry W. Whelchel was the contingent beneficiary.

Andrew stuck his head in the office, "Ladies, let me know if you need anything. I'm just down the hall."

Laura looked up and smiled. "I've found a few files you may want to look through. If you don't mind, I'll bring them to your office before we leave."

"Of course. That will be fine. Hey, don't worry about straightening up in here, the cleaning crew will take care of that later in the week."

When Laura and Julia completed going through Henry's office, Julia left for home, and Laura stopped by Andrew's office to give him the files she had mentioned to him earlier.

"Andrew, these files, except for this one, are all work-related. Please look at the contents of the file with SSR on the front, and we will discuss it later. I've also included a copy of Henry's paystub. It appears his salary was direct deposited into two bank accounts. The first account listed is our household account, but I don't recognize the second account. There's a thousand dollars of his paycheck going to a bank account I don't recognize. Could you find out where that money is going?"

****

Laura had promised Fitz that she would check on Mia when she finished at the law firm. She stopped by the hospital cafeteria on the main floor and grabbed a coffee and a muffin before going to the ICU area.

Laura checked in at the nurses' station when she entered the unit, and they told her that Fitz arrived an hour earlier. As she walked toward Mia's bay, she overheard Fitz speaking in Italian, and as Laura got closer, she saw he was talking to someone on the phone.

Laura studied French in school and knew enough words in Italian to order in a restaurant, if the waiter was patient and of good humor.

She once again heard a somber tone emerging during his conversation. It was apparent Fitz had tried to hide that side of him from her, and perhaps from Julia, too. She had a suspicious feeling that all was not on the level with Fitz Romano.

Fitz finished his call. "Hi, Laura. How are you?"

"I'm well, thank you. What are you up to?"

"Just finished a business call. Mom's been in and out of consciousness all morning. But she's enjoyed several lucid moments since I arrived."

"That's a good sign, Fitz."

"Well, yeah, but she's struggling to tell me something that seems important. If she could stay awake for longer than a few minutes, it would be helpful."

"Did Julia know you were coming up this morning?"

"No."

"She went with me to Henry's office this morning before going back home. Julia's working the afternoon shift. But I'm certain she would have come by had she known you were here."

"I didn't tell Julia I was coming back this morning, because after my visit with Mom, I planned to stop by and talk with you about something."

"Sure, Fitz. I'll be home in about an hour, so come on by when you get ready."

Laura left the Intensive Care Unit in a hurry. She had a feeling that Fitz planned to ask her permission to marry Julia.

Laura suddenly realized Mia knew it was time to tell her son the truth about his father.

As she left the hospital and headed toward her car, she thought about how her girls would respond to the news. Henry's illicit affair and the story of his illegitimate son would taint the sweet memory of their father.

Just then, her phone rang, and it was Betsy.

Good Lord, I just don't think I can bear to speak with her now.

The phone went silent. Laura felt a sense of relief, but it didn't last long because the phone rang again. She knew better than to ignore the second call.

Laura got into her car and then answered the phone. The Bluetooth engaged as she secured the seatbelt.

"Hello, Betsy. How are you, sweetie?"

Betsy started screaming into the phone as she told her mother that Hal found out about her affair with the personal trainer. He insisted she pack her things and be out of the house by the time he got home from work. She was sobbing hysterically.

Laura lowered her voice and spoke slowly as she said, "Sweetheart, what are you going to do?"

"I'm on my way to your house until Hal calms down."

"What!"

"Now, do you understand? You can't sell the house, Mom, because I need a place to live."

"Sweetie, where are you?" Laura asked.

"I'm driving on the interstate, why?"

"I need you to pull off at the next exit. Find a fast-food restaurant nearby. I'll hold while you find a place to park."

Laura leaned back against the headrest and closed her eyes as she gathered her thoughts on how to help Betsy through this crisis.

Déjà vu, all over again. This is the same conversation my mom had with me many years ago.

"Okay, Mom, I'm parked."

"Now listen to me. Remember, ten years ago, Hal could not wait to marry you," Laura reasoned. "I'm sure you and Hal will work things out, as soon as he settles down and gets his facts sorted out."

"Mom, did you not hear me say I'm having an affair with my personal trainer?"

"Honey, do you love Hal?" Laura asked.

"Of course, I love him. But he works such long hours, and he's always tired," Betsy sobbed. "He doesn't touch me anymore, Mom. He never even looks at me."

Laura considered how to explain the logic of her waiting for Hal to get home from work before making any rash decisions.

She knew Henry would just tell her to go back home and stay in the house.

Hal should be the one to leave.

"Well, let me tell you how to handle this situation. Turn around and go back home."

"Mom, please."

"Hear me out, Betsy," Laura said. "Turn around and go back home and wait until Hal returns from work. Send the boys away from the house so you guys can talk. Then, explain to Hal that you love him, and you recognize that he is an excellent father and provider, but let him know that you have needs, too. Just tell him you miss the intimacy that you once enjoyed, and that you need him to be the man you fell in love with."

"Mom, do you realize how lame that sounds?" Betsy asked.

"Well, it's worth a try, honey. This isn't an ideal situation to be in. Still, you have two sons to consider, and Hal is likely to return home from work this afternoon with a different attitude than when he left this morning."

"I don't know, Mom. He's livid with me."

"Betsy, if you aren't there when he gets home from work, he'll think you no longer love him and that you have given up on your marriage. Now turn that car around and get back to your family. And Betsy..."

"Yes, ma'am?"

"Remember, honey, it's your responsibility to keep your family together. I love you, and I'll be praying that you can work this out."

"Mom, that's a lot of pressure to put on me."

"No, honey, when you married Hal and gave birth to those boys, you put that pressure on yourself. Now, I need to go. I've got another call coming in."

Laura disconnected the call with Betsy, took a deep breath, and answered the next call.

"Daisy, how are you? It's so good to hear your voice."

"I've decided to cook dinner tonight," Daisy said. "Can you come over around six?"

"Yes, I would love to. I'll be there at 6:00."

When Laura hung up, she knew she should go home, wait for Fitz to come by, and perhaps Betsy, too. Instead, she remembered needing to shop for a few items. And she headed to the mall.

****

Later in the evening, when the meal ended, Daisy went into the kitchen to plate the dessert. Andrew lowered his voice as he peeked through the door to make sure Daisy would not overhear their conversation. "Perhaps you should call me tomorrow. I have some news about the documents you left in my office earlier today."

He looked back toward the kitchen. "Also, the investigative report confirmed the family's involvement in a Columbian drug cartel."

Laura closed her eyes as she shook her head in resignation.

Chapter Twenty-Two

Laura poured the last of the coffee into her mug and walked into the study to place the dreaded call to Andrew about the contents of the envelopes she gave him to research.

"Hi Laura, thanks for calling. I've reviewed the documents you left for me yesterday."

"Okay. What did you find out? Which bank was Henry using?"

"The money was deposited into a bank account in Macon, Georgia." There was silence on the other line as Andrew waited for Laura to respond.

"Also, the insurance policy that you found has lapsed from lack of payment. I'm sorry, Laura. I know you were hoping this would turn out differently."

Laura recovered from the immediate shock. Although she admitted it was an uncomfortable situation for Andrew, she asked if he'd known about the existence of Sofia Suarez Romano.

Andrew got up from his desk, walked over to the window, and stood for a few moments.

"Yes. I must admit that I found out by accident many years ago." He turned from the window and leaned against a bookshelf.

"The Law School at Mercer University in Macon invited me to speak to a class of students. Daisy went with me." He paused as he rubbed the area between his eyes.

"Go ahead, Andrew."

"On Friday evening following the talk, I took Daisy out to dinner. We went to that little Italian restaurant on State Highway 19, they changed the name to Duane Allman Boulevard. I know you've heard Henry speak of the restaurant."

"Yes, he mentioned that restaurant to me."

"When we walked into the restaurant, I glanced around and saw Henry dining with a beautiful young woman. And at that moment, he reached over and kissed her. I remember Henry was out of the office that Friday, but when I saw them at the table, I knew he wasn't there on business."

Andrew sighed as he walked back to his desk.

"Of course, I hadn't made reservations. You know, it's a popular restaurant and the wait time was long. So, I turned to Daisy and told her I didn't want to wait forty-five minutes to eat dinner. We left the restaurant without Henry noticing us, or without Daisy seeing Henry and the other woman."

Laura's bottom lip quivered as she wiped the tears from her eyes.

Andrew chuckled. "Had Daisy seen Henry kiss that woman, she would have walked right up to him and slapped his face! You know how much she cherishes your friendship."

Laura smiled.

"Does Daisy know?"

"No. I told no one."

"Thank you, Andrew. You were a loyal friend to both of us, and I appreciate your honesty. I realize Henry's death has been hard on you, too."

****

Later that same day Marsha walked through the back door and looked around the quiet kitchen.

"Mom, where are you?"

"I'm back here, darling," Laura said. "I'm in my sitting room."

Marsha grabbed a bottled water from the fridge and then walked toward her parent's suite. She noticed the house was spotless, even though several empty boxes were stacked in the foyer.

"Mom, what's up with these boxes? Are you packing up Dad's stuff?"

"Not yet, darling. I was hoping you girls would help me sort through his things."

"I'll be glad to help you. Perhaps, we could get started this weekend."

Later, Marsha sat at the bar and enjoyed a glass of wine while Laura warmed up their dinner.

"I met with Andrew again this morning."

"How's Andrew?"

"He's well."

Laura hesitated as she fidgeted with the pad on the counter.

"I thought you should know, I've asked him to complete a background check on Fitz."

"What are you talking about, Mom?"

"I'm concerned about his line of work."

"So? You're inquisitive," Marsha said. "What difference does that make?"

"I've asked Andrew to investigate Fitz. Just to be sure nothing illegal is going on."

"You can't just investigate one of our boyfriends. You've got to stop being a helicopter mom. We're way too old for that kind of parental involvement."

"Please calm down. I didn't mean to get you all up in arms," Laura said. "I sometimes forget how analytical you are."

"Mom, at our age, why would you investigate anyone we dated? Did you and Dad investigate Hal before Betsy married him?"

"No! We had no reason to."

"Then I'm confused about why you felt it was necessary. I could see Dad doing something like that when we were sixteen. But Julia's a thirty-two-year-old divorcee, and she's a nurse practitioner. Lord knows, she's not stupid."

"Now, Marsha, please calm down," Laura said. "I never said your sister was stupid. You know I would never even consider such a thought."

Marsha sighed.

"Please let me explain. I heard two phone conversations while Fitz was staying here. And I overheard another conversation today at the hospital. In each situation, he spoke in a foreign language with an authoritative, mean-spirited tone. It was unlike a typical discussion a successful salesperson would have with a customer. During all three conversations, darkness emerged from his personality that caused me concern."

"So, you think he's involved in criminal activity?" Marsha asked.

"The investigative report confirms Mia's Colombian family runs a drug cartel in the States," Laura explained. "And, yes, I believe Fitz may be involved, that frightens me for Julia, and the rest of us."

"Holy crap! What is she thinking?"

"Honey, I'm not sure Julia even knows about the cartel. But, when the FBI questioned her about the people staying here the weekend they found the body in the creek, she never mentioned Fitz."

Marsha poured another glass of wine and paced around the kitchen as she thought out loud. "Mom, this is not only serious, but dangerous. Suppose Julia knows about the cartel, and she deliberately withheld Fitz's name from the FBI."

"Honey, it appears she knows something," Laura said. "Why else would she leave his name off the list?"

"Are you expecting Julia and Betsy this weekend?"

"Julia, yes, Betsy, no. She and Hal are having problems."

"I've suspected that since before Dad died," Marsha said. "Remember the many outbursts we've witnessed since Dad's funeral. We knew something was up. And, most notably, was her insistence that Hal should deliver the family eulogy."

"Well, you were right," Laura said. "Apparently, your sister had an affair with her personal trainer. Perhaps her marital problems are responsible for her recent outbursts, besides the grief of losing your father."

"Mom, how do you keep from falling apart? Every time we talk, you are dealing with yet another family crisis. Has it always been like this?" Marsha asked.

"Honey, when you have children, there is never a dull moment."

"Maybe hiring investigators is necessary when you're a mother of three girls."

Laura smiled.

"Sorry, that upsets you, sweetheart," Laura said. "But I have to protect my family."

"I didn't tell you, but I plan to stay for the weekend. So, hopefully, I can get Julia to tell me more about Fitz's profession. We've got to make sure she doesn't get hurt."

Chapter Twenty-Three

Julia worked the morning shift and drove straight from work to her mom's house in time to enjoy dinner with her mother and sister. Her stomach rumbled with pangs of hunger. Remembering she hadn't eaten since breakfast, she was now craving chips, salsa, and margaritas.

Julia entered through the kitchen door and walked toward the sound of music playing. At the other end of the house, she found her mother and Marsha sorting through her dad's clothes. Marsha and Laura had spent the day cleaning out Henry's closet. She stopped and looked from one to another.

"What are you guys doing?"

"Your sister suggested cleaning out Henry's closet this weekend."

Julia walked over and picked up a familiar shirt from a stack on the chair. She closed her eyes as she breathed in the smell.

"This is a shirt I gave to Dad one year for Christmas. I remember him putting it on as soon as he opened it."

Julia smiled.

"Dad was just like that, you know. It wasn't enough that he said, thank you. He'd try it on and just wear it for the rest of the day."

Tears formed in her eyes as she saw his golf bag sitting next to the door.

Then, she turned toward her mother and hugged her, "I'm glad we're staying the weekend. No one should have to do this alone."

Laura wiped her eyes and said, "What do you ladies want for dinner tonight? We could grill a steak or cook a piece of salmon and make a salad."

"To be honest, Mom, I've been craving Mexican all day."

"I could go for some Mexican food," Marsha said. "But how about we pick it up and bring it back here. We've got a lot of work to get done before we go to bed tonight."

"Well, I'm taking my suitcase upstairs, and when I come back down, I'll go pick up our order while you finish up here?"

"Good idea," Marsha said.

"Marsha, while I'm gone," Julia said. "How about you make a batch of your frozen margaritas?"

When Julia walked into the bedroom, she smiled when she saw the covers on the bed folded down, showing her mother had put clean linens on her bed. All that her mom had on her plate today, and she took the time to spruce up her room. There was a small bouquet of flowers sitting on the nightstand, and a few magazines for Julia to enjoy over the weekend.

During dinner, Julia and Marsha took turns telling stories about their father. Many of the stories caused cries of laughter, but their memories also conjured up a few stories that triggered tears.

Julia said, "Mom, I hope Dad realized how much we loved him."

"Of course, he did."

"The thing I remember most about our childhood, is that we never knew when you two were going through a rocky patch in your marriage."

"As you well know, my dear, time tests all marriages. But, what I've wanted most for you girls was to find a good man who would love and protect you. I pray that prayer every day."

Julia and Marsha went back into the suite to tidy up their project and removed the items that remained, so their mom could sleep in her bed. While they were working, Marsha filled Julia in about Betsy's marital problems.

"Mom's still praying for us, Marsha. She's not giving up, is she?"

"Nope, she'll never give up on us until she takes her last breath."

When Julia and Marsha went upstairs to get ready for bed, Julia hugged her sister and went into her room and closed the door.

She pulled the suitcase over and lifted it onto the bed. It seemed heavier than it should, considering she only brought pajamas and a pair of jeans, a sweatshirt, a button-down shirt, and a pair of leggings. Julia unzipped the top, and her mouth flew open. Bundles of hundred-dollar bills filled the suitcase. When she finished counting, Julia performed a quick calculation and realized there were one million dollars in cash stuffed in the suitcase.

Chapter Twenty-Four

Julia sat down on the floor beside her bed and retraced her steps from the evening before. She packed the suitcase while waiting for Fitz to come over for dinner. He, too, had planned a quick trip with friends, and he would check on his mom at the hospital throughout the weekend. Fitz came in rolling his suitcase and asked what to use to clean the dirt from the wheels. After he finished cleaning it, he moved it next to her luggage, but she couldn't remember which side he had left it.

Julia put her hands over her face and wondered how to approach Fitz about the suitcase. Her natural first instinct was to call him, but to do so could cause a problem. And she didn't want to mess up their relationship because they were getting along so well.

The discovery heightened her suspense about what she had wondered: *What is it precisely that Fitz does for a living?*

He told her he worked from home, but he didn't even have a home office. He drove a luxury vehicle, and he lived in a high-end apartment.

She googled his name several times. However, she had been unsuccessful in finding any documented work history.

Julia got up on the bed and covered her face with the pillow that smelled of lavender. She shivered as she considered that having the suitcase in her possession could make her an accessory to some type of illegal activity. She contemplated going to talk to her mom, and then she thought that it was perhaps too much information for her mother.

When Julia's phone rang, it was Fitz. She hesitated to answer, but knew he would just call her mother if she didn't answer. She picked up the phone, and he told her he'd just left the hospital.

"Hi, Babe. Listen, I need to come by and swap suitcases with you. I love those cute little pajamas you packed, but they aren't my color, you know what I mean?"

She didn't know how to explain that she knew about the money in the suitcase, so she just played along. "Oh. So, you must have mistaken my luggage for your own when you left last night. I wasn't paying attention."

"No worries. We probably should find a way to distinguish one from the other, huh? But listen, just take my luggage, put it in the back seat of your car, and leave the car unlocked. I should be there in less than ten minutes to make the exchange."

"Well, you could come inside Fitz, and say hello."

"Not tonight, I don't want to disturb your mother this late. I'll see you later. Thanks for doing this. Talk soon."

When Julia was sure the contents looked perfect, she zipped the suitcase and went downstairs and followed Fitz's instructions. Julia tip-toed through the house, being careful not to make any noises.

The last thing she needed was for her mom to come out of her suite and ask about her late-night luggage swap. Julia knew her mother, and the interrogation would be hell until she opened the luggage and revealed the contents.

Julia waited in the dark parlor until she saw Fitz's car lights leave the garage area. Then she slipped outside the kitchen door, where she removed her luggage from the same spot she had left Fitz's earlier.

When Julia lifted it from the car, she recognized it was hers because it was much lighter. She slipped back inside the house and tip-toed back up to her room without making a sound.

Placing her luggage on the bed, she unzipped it and found a long-stem red rose pinned to her pajamas with a note that read, "I'll think about you tonight wearing these cute PJs."

Chapter Twenty-Five

Over breakfast Saturday morning, Julia asked Marsha if she wanted to ride horses later in the day.

After they finished packing up their dad's belongings, they changed into their riding clothes.

Marsha drove the Gator down to the stable. At the same time, Julia planned a hypothetical situation about finding a suitcase stuffed with money. She'd rehearsed several versions of the story throughout the night. Still, now that she was in Marsha's presence, Julia realized that her sister was way too smart, and would find the immediate holes in her story.

But, once they got to the stable, Marsha brought up various topics, one of which was Fitz.

"Tell me again, what is it that Fitz does? Did you say he was in sales?" Marsha asked.

"Yes. Fitz is a salesman."

"What is it he sells? Does he deal with finances or commodities, or is he one of those infamous Amway Soap dealers?"

They both laughed.

"No, I think he's like a financial advisor. You know, Marsha, he's self-employed and doesn't discuss his clients, and being in the medical field, I don't discuss mine either. So, we tend not to talk about our careers much. There are more interesting things to talk about than work."

"Well, be careful, Julia. Sometimes, when men are deceptive about their careers, it's because they are hiding some illegal activity."

A sudden wave of paranoia swept over Julia. She wondered if Marsha had heard her moving around the house the previous night. She was careful in her reaction to her sister's comment.

"Thanks, Marsha." And with a casual wave of her hand, Julia said, "It's all good."

When they finished their ride, they brushed their horses, fed them, and then got back on the Gator to head back to the house.

As they crested the hill, a strange car was coming up the rear-drive towards the garage. Julia saw that the signage on the door was a courier service that she had recognized from the city.

Marsha drove up to the courier and lowered her window. "Can we help you?"

The driver of the vehicle looked up and said, "Yes, ma'am. I have a delivery for Fitz Romano, in care of Julia McKenzie. Is either of you Julia?"

"That would be me," Julia said.

He took the package around to Julia and asked for her signature on the black box.

"There must be a valuable piece of jewelry in that box. They insured it for a quarter of a million dollars," the driver said with a chuckle.

Appalled that the driver would comment on the package he delivered, Julia shook her head in disbelief. "How do you know the amount of insurance?"

"It says right there on the label. Insurance limits up to a quarter a million dollars," the driver responded.

Marsha rolled her eyes as she cranked the Gator and drove back into the garage, leaving Julia alone with the driver.

Julia laughed.

"That means your courier service offers insurance coverage for up to that amount. And to be clear, you should not be commenting on the packages you deliver. I'm surprised your supervisor didn't cover that minor detail during your training."

"Well, excuse me. I don't work for the courier service. I just borrowed my friend's car to make this delivery. So, I didn't realize there were rules and regulations involved. Anyway, you've got the package, and I'll text the guy and let him know."

"Since you're not an official employee of the courier service, let me have the number of the guy you are texting with that information," Julia said.

"Okay. What the hell. The number is 080-297-6133."

Julia punched the number in her phone on her way into the house. She went straight up to her bedroom and locked the door. As her mind raced about the contents, Julia looked for a smooth surface to place the box. Then she remembered the seamless granite surface in the bathroom.

She took great care while peeling the tape back from the outer layer of brown paper. With the tape removed, and a gentle nudge, she pulled the box out from under the wrapping and lifted the top. There were six bags of a white powdery substance that could pass for baking soda. Still, she knew that was not what was in the bag.

While she was securing the package, she heard a knock on her bedroom door and Marsha yelled, "Julia, what are you doing in there? Fitz is downstairs, waiting on you."

"I had to go to the bathroom! I'll be down in a minute."

Julia's hands trembled as she inspected the box. Then, she washed her hands and went downstairs to greet Fitz.

He was sitting at the bar, talking to Laura about his mother's condition. She overheard him say that he came by the house on Monday afternoon as they agreed, but she wasn't home.

Fitz wore a casual pair of khaki slacks and a golf shirt, he looked as if he planned to play a round of golf with friends later in the day. But she couldn't remember him ever mentioning playing golf in the past.

It was normal for them to hug when seeing each other, but this time Julia kept her distance.

After a few moments, Laura excused herself. She winked at Julia and went back to her suite to continue her cleanout of Henry's belongings.

She could've stayed a moment longer. Julia thought. *Maybe she thought we wanted to be alone to talk.*

Fitz lowered his voice, "Just so you know, there is a courier service scheduled to deliver a package addressed to me, within the next fifteen minutes. I hope you don't mind me having it delivered to you. I wasn't sure where I would be today, and I knew you would be here all weekend."

Julia smiled.

"Sure," Julia said. "They delivered the package over an hour ago. It's upstairs in my room. I'll run up and get it."

When she came back down, she handed the package to Fitz.

"Here it is. Are you staying for dinner?" Julia asked.

"I've got to meet someone at the Atlanta airport in a few hours. If I don't run into much traffic, maybe I could come back." Seeing the disappointment on Julia's face, Fitz said, "If not, I'll come in the morning in time to go to church with you."

"You know, don't bother coming tomorrow morning. We've promised Mom, that we'd finish cleaning out Dad's stuff, and we had not planned on going to church. Perhaps, you should spend tomorrow with your mom instead."

Chapter Twenty-Six

On Tuesday morning, Laura received a call from Theo Williams. He explained that the buyer of the property suggested a new contract to include the inventory and machinery. He wanted the transaction to be all-inclusive, as opposed to showing one price for the farm and another price for the farm equipment. Theo explained there was one caveat. The buyer wanted to take possession of the property on Thursday afternoon, before the closing on Friday at noon. But the buyer also agreed to wire the funds to Laura's account before the close of business on Thursday.

Laura drove into town to meet Theo at his office and sign the revised contract.

Once the signing was done, Laura sat back in her chair and sighed.

"Well, Theo, thank you for helping me with this sale. I don't know what I would've done without your expertise."

"No problem. In all honesty, Laura, this has been one of the easiest sales that I have ever handled. Remember, it was like this buyer came out of nowhere and made an offer. How often does that happen?" Theo asked.

"Tell me, Theo, is there a demand in the market for a house of my size? Now that the farm has sold, I just don't have the energy or the desire to maintain a large house anymore."

Theo looked at Laura and said, "Are you doing okay, Laura?"

"Yes, I'm getting used to a new normal, so to speak. At first, I thought I would rather die than leave my home, but the longer I stay, the more I realize the advantage of selling and living off the returns from my investments."

"I understand that point of view. If you like, I'll get out there in a day or two and start assessing the value, and we'll create a video of your home to put up on the website. We've found that people are more interested in viewing a video of a house before scheduling a visit."

Laura reached for her pocketbook and prepared to leave Theo's office.

"Laura, may I suggest going down to the barn before Thursday to remove anything personal or any items you don't want to leave behind."

"Sure, I'll take care of it."

"Be sure and get the tax returns," Theo said. "I remember them being in the top drawer of the filing cabinet when I was last down there with Henry. It would also be a good idea to clean out the desk in the small office."

The next morning, Laura changed into her jeans and farm boots and took the Gator out to the road, which led to the barn. Although she had insisted Henry pave the way from the main highway down to their house, the sparse covered graveled road which led to the barn and stable was a one-lane dirt road. Since their farm was no longer a working farm, there was seldom any traffic going down to the barn. Today, however, as she rounded the first curve, she was met by a white eighteen-wheeler with no signage other than the prominent display of a DOT Number.

In a quick reaction, Laura swerved the Gator to allow the tractor-trailer to get by, but the cab had just avoided hitting her. She turned the steering wheel so hard that the impact caused an immediate stop by the Gator. Laura turned to look for further identification on the truck, but it had already rounded the curve, and was out of sight.

The Gator's position was sitting at a perpendicular angle. Laura got off and pushed it back onto the dirt road as she wondered what that truck was doing on her property.

The buyer was scheduled to come to the farm for the walkthrough around three o'clock, but Laura intended to complete her clean-out long before that time. Yet, this little venture had taken up a good twenty minutes.

Unnerved, Laura's hands shook as she grasped the steering wheel.

She had always felt the farm, with the large patches of hardwoods and pine trees, had insulated her home against unwanted traffic and was secure from the outside world. There was one road in, and once you got on the farm, there was no other way out, unless one left on foot.

When Laura opened the barn's side door, she detected a movement, as she entered the small room.

Laura hesitated as she stood in the middle of the office.

The movement could've been a shadow, or perhaps the wind caused the curtain to move. Goodness, I've got work to do here...

The small office housed a desk, chair, and filing cabinet. But then she detected a smell unfamiliar to the barn.

Laura sat in the office and searched the drawers and files, looking for anything unrelated to the sale. As she looked at each piece of paper, she either trashed it or placed it on the desk to preserve for the new owners. There was one file inside the desk drawer containing the original Bills of Sale of all the farm equipment they had purchased throughout the years.

Henry made copies of the Bills of Sale to keep with the appropriate years' tax returns. Still, the originals were in the desk. As expected, the top drawer of the filing cabinet stored the tax returns for the farm, dating back ten years. Laura carefully removed the files and transferred them to an empty box she found under the desk. After she cleaned out the first drawer, she opened the second, third, and fourth, but they were empty. She couldn't understand who'd been down there because the drawers had been full of files and assorted tools. Then, she went back to the desk and checked once more to make sure she removed all unnecessary clutter.

Before taking the box of files outside, she walked into the barn and saw what seemed to be hundreds of pallets of cellophane-wrapped bundles that took up half the floor space.

This must be what I smelled when I opened the door.

Laura reached for her cell phone to call Theo when she heard a sound from outside the barn. The call went straight to voicemail, but she left a quick message asking Theo to meet her at the barn office at his earliest convenience. Then, Laura went back into the office and grabbed the box of files, and headed outside to the Gator.

She looked around the side of the barn and didn't see anyone. A gush of wind caused a creaking sound from the old barn, which she thought could have caused the earlier sound of movement. Then she went back inside the office to wait for Theo's call.

Thirty minutes or more passed, and Laura continued to check the phone messages. Considering the barn's cell service was sporadic on a good day, she feared she would miss Theo's call. Laura's nerves were on edge as she paced around the office and thought about her near accident.

Was the tractor-trailer that ran me off the road earlier responsible for the large pallets stored in the barn?

Laura looked at her watch again. She wondered what was keeping Theo.

He can contact the potential buyers and find out if they were expecting a shipment.

Laura sat at the desk and waited. The quiet barn was unnerving, so she opened the door.

When Laura stepped outside, a dark shadow jumped from behind the door, placed a cloth over her head, and someone else grabbed her hands and tied them with zip ties. She tried to scream, but the fabric was so tight around her face that it would've been impossible to open her mouth.

Chapter Twenty-Seven

Her captors guided her to an old tree stump on the backside of the barn, and sat her on it. They explained what they planned to do to her if she told anyone about what she saw inside.

The broken English they used was hard to understand, but she got the idea. It was quite simple. She and her daughters would die if she talked. They were graphic in their explanation, as they wouldn't just kill them, they could expect a slow, agonizing death.

As they continued to detail their torture, one man lifted the cloth and removed the diamond earrings from her ears, and replaced them with a pair of hoop earrings.

"You keep these things in your ears and never take them out. It tells me where you go and what you say," The leader said.

To show her they meant business; one man knocked her around as shock and horror pierced through her body. Because of the head covering, she couldn't see the next blow coming. When the man's fist landed above her eye, the pain exploded across her face.

She saw stars.

Liquid droplets appeared on her lips. The metal taste from the blood terrified her, and she feared for her life.

A second guy jerked her shirt open and ripped it partially off with his calloused hands. She tensed up in fear of what might happen next.

Unconsciously, she chewed the inside of her cheek as the crisp air moved against her exposed torso. Her breathing was hard and fast, and she thought she might hyperventilate.

Oh, my God. These savages are going to rape me right here in broad daylight.

Then, another captor brushed her side while removing the head covering as he walked past, and a few seconds later, she heard the barn door close behind her.

The men wore dark shades. Their homemade facemasks, constructed from blue and white bandanas, covered most of their faces and allowed them to speak freely.

When the leader returned, he came from the back of the barn and spoke in a rapid Spanish dialect. Laura had studied several foreign languages throughout her youth. Before a two-week vacation to Spain, she took a crash course in Spanish. Still, the dialect spoken by the men was unfamiliar to her.

It was apparent they were using slang, which confused her about what they were discussing. They exchanged a few words in a language she did not recognize, and she measured the leader's obvious anger by the pitch of his voice. It was apparent he was telling the guy to leave her alone. Still, the guy refused to obey the command.

She sensed an increase of tension in the air, then the leader produced a machete from behind his back and aimed it in her direction. There was a precision to his swift swing that cut through the air and connected with his target. As Laura gasped in horror, the man's calloused hands fell limp and left her body as his severed head rolled across the ground. Although horrified and in a state of shock, she was thankful the man was no longer touching her.

"Cover her head," the leader said.

They were quick to follow his instruction.

Then he said, "This is what happens when you don't follow my instructions." He directed the two other men to clean up the mess, as if the dead body was nothing more than a random piece of garbage. Once they removed the body, he turned to Laura and said, "You aren't to speak a word to anyone. Do you understand? Otherwise, great harm will come to your daughters. You are not to tell anyone what has happened here today."

Laura questioned the sanity of that command.

What is he thinking?

It made no sense. They were leaving Laura tied to a tree stump, and if someone were to find her, the first question would be about her blood-splattered clothes and the cut above her eye.

Then there was the question about the large puddle of blood on the ground.

And how does he know about my girls?

However, she knew she must tell no one because the consequences would be grave.

The extreme heat from the mid-morning sun caused a profuse sweat underneath the cloth covering her head. Laura sat as still as she could, to avoid calling attention to herself. But the sound of her heart beating echoed in her ears.

She could hear the buzzing of insects swarming above the large puddle of blood that lay near her feet. Surprised, Laura felt her senses heighten. She knew the men might still be watching her, but she lost control of her emotions.

The tears flowed.

Finally, Laura detected a familiar smell and heard someone approaching. Then, someone lifted her arm and spoke. She recognized the leader's voice.

"Stand up," he said. "I'm gonna help you back into the barn."

As he opened the door to the office, he cut the ties from her hands. "Now step inside," he said, "and wait five minutes before you remove the cover from your head. Then walk outside and get in your vehicle and go back up to your house. Do not look back down here. Never come back to this barn ever again. If you do, neither you nor any member of your family will live to tell about it. Do you understand what I'm saying?"

Laura opened her mouth, but she couldn't speak.

She nodded in agreement.

Chapter Twenty-Eight

When Laura got back to her house, she ran inside and turned on the security system. She delayed the movement scanner for three minutes, which allowed enough time to grab a Diet Coke from the fridge and get to the master suite bathroom, the only room in the house not wired for security.

Laura removed the tattered and bloodied clothes and jumped into the shower, turning the lever to the hottest setting she could tolerate, and scrubbed the blood from her body. She lathered her hair and fiercely rubbed her scalp with her nails. As the shampoo and water ran down her face, the abrasions on her forehead began to sting. She reached for a towel from the outside shelf of the open shower stall.

After the morning experience at the barn, she could never again imagine living alone in the house. Without realizing how long she had been in the shower, the water cooled, so she cut it off and patted the cut above her eye with a dry rag before drying herself off.

Laura spent more time than usual as she applied her makeup, careful to cover the abrasions and cuts on her upper torso and face.

When she blow-dried her hair, she styled her hair with side bangs to keep the worst cut over her eye from being so noticeable. As Laura aged, her blonde hair had begun to thin, and if anyone looked too closely, they would see the mark left by the guy who assaulted her. But with great skill, she concealed and applied makeup, which hid it from view.

When Laura heard the phone on the vanity ring, she froze. Then, she grabbed a hand towel and picked up the phone but said nothing.

Finally, Theo said, "Laura, is that you? Please pick up."

"Theo. So sorry for the delay. How are you?"

"Hi Laura, I'm fine. You asked me to call you at my earliest convenience. I've been in a loan closing all morning, and I decided to grab a bite of lunch before heading your way. And it's a good thing because I just got off the phone with the buyer's attorney. There has been a change in schedule. We will meet at Andrew's office to sign the papers. The buyer will meet at the same time at his attorney's office and sign. We will then fax the signature page to the other party. Once everyone has signed, the attorneys will send the original documents by courier to the other attorneys for signature, and we keep that original document."

Laura said, "I've never heard of faxing papers back and forth, but if Andrew is okay with the agreement, then I am, too."

"These types of signings are often necessary. Mostly when the buyer and seller are in different cities." Theo said, "this saves travel time, and I didn't think you would mind this slight deviation from the schedule. Also, the four o'clock walkthrough, scheduled for this afternoon, is no longer needed. The agent canceled it."

"When do we go to Andrew's office for the signing?"

"At ten o'clock on Friday morning. However, the money will wire to your bank account tomorrow afternoon. So, if there's anything in the barn you want to keep, go get it this afternoon. Is that possible?"

"I've already done it."

When Laura hung up the phone, she heard the doorbell. Holding her trembling hands, she walked into the bathroom and closed the door.

Her cell phone pinged. There was a text from Marsha.

<Mom, the door's locked, and the alarm is engaged. Are you home?>

Laura's hands shook as she replied. <Yes, be out in a minute. Come on in.>

She punched in her alarm code to turn off the system, then took one more look in the mirror, careful to pull her bangs down over her eyebrow. She took a deep breath and walked out of her suite into the foyer.

"Marsha, darling, this is such a pleasant surprise. I wasn't expecting you today."

Marsha explained that she contacted Julia and Betsy, and they had agreed to come home and spend a few days before the closing on the property.

"We want to spend some time this weekend riding our horses. Maybe you'll ride with us since this will be our last time."

As Marsha talked about riding, Laura felt perspiration streaming down her spine. The killer's threat rang in her ears.

Trying to dismiss the thought, she saw Julia's car pulling into the circular driveway. Betsy was sitting on the passenger's side.

Julia and Betsy came inside the house talking about horseback riding.

Laura thought it was the only reason they'd come home, but she had to think of a way to stop them from going anywhere near the barn.

"Why don't you girls freshen up and afterward we'll go to the club for an early dinner? I haven't been over there in months, and it will give us a chance to catch up."

"Mom's right," Marsha said. "Besides, it's getting hot outside, and we have plenty of time to ride. I'd rather stay here this afternoon, enjoy a light dinner at the house, and perhaps go for a horseback ride early tomorrow morning."

Laura found a large piece of salmon in the freezer and laid it out on the counter to thaw.

"Julia, you know a lot about wine selection. How about going down to the cellar and grab a few bottles to pair with the salmon? I'll toss a salad before we grill the fish."

The phone rang, and Laura reached for it as she pulled the lettuce from the crisper. She talked for a few minutes, and as soon as Julia returned with the wine, she said, "Listen up, girls. That was Rhett Louis, your father's financial advisor. He'll be here tomorrow morning at 10 o'clock to discuss Henry's portfolio."

Betsy helped set the dinner table while Julia chilled the wine and got down four wine glasses. Then, she gathered the ingredients to make her grandmother's homemade salad dressing.

While the girls were busy, Laura slipped out of the kitchen. After a few minutes, Marsha became concerned and began looking for her mom.

Chapter Twenty-Nine

Standing in the doorway of her father's study, Marsha watched her mother pour a drink from the liquor cabinet. Laura turned and asked, "Is dinner ready?"

"Not yet," Marsha answered. "The wine needs to chill a bit longer. Do you mind if we sit a moment and enjoy a drink while they finish making the salad dressing?"

"Of course not, darling." She said as she placed a few sticks of wood in the fireplace.

Marsha noticed a slight smile on her mom's face for the first time since she arrived. She couldn't help but wonder what had caused her mother's lousy disposition throughout the afternoon.

"Help yourself to a drink, dear."

"Are you planning to start a fire before dinner, Mom?"

"No. But I thought we might enjoy one later in the evening," Laura said as she self-consciously swept her bangs away from her eyes.

Marsha noticed something different about her mom's hair. However, she couldn't quite put her finger on it.

And there it was. When her mother moved a strand of hair as she sipped her drink, there was blood-soaked makeup caked to the right of her temple. Careful not to let her mother know she had seen the abrasion, she moved to the chair near the fireplace to get a better look.

Marsha motioned for Laura to sit on the sofa as she turned and opened the cabinet behind the chair. Searching for a snack, she removed a tin of cashews and held them in the air, "Dad always kept snacks in here for us to enjoy. Would you like some cashews?" Marsha poured a handful of nuts into Laura's shaking palms, but she didn't mention it because she was looking at the marks on her mother's face and wrists.

"Mom, where did that blood come from on your head?" Marsha asked.

Laura lifted her shaky hand to her forehead. "Oh, it's nothing. I slipped and fell earlier this morning."

Marsha sat down in the chair across from her mother and sipped her drink. When Laura reached for a few more nuts, Marsha saw what looked like rope burns and fresh bruising on her wrists.

Wonder what actually happened. A simple fall wouldn't cause those places on her wrists.

She asked no more questions as she sat in silence and let her mother enjoy her drink.

Julia yelled that dinner was ready.

During dinner, Laura made several blunders trying to serve the salmon from the platter. Her difficulty was so severe at one point that the serving utensils slipped from her hands.

"Oh, by the way, Rhett Louis called earlier in the day and scheduled to come by at ten o'clock in the morning to discuss Henry's portfolio."

Julia shot a sideways glance at Marsha.

"Mom, really? We were all here when he called this afternoon," Betsy said.

Laura looked at Marsha for confirmation.

"Don't worry, Mom. We'll be here all weekend. We can make time to meet with him. It won't cause a problem for any of us."

Later in the evening, after the girls had cleaned up the kitchen, Marsha smelled a fire burning and knew her mother had ignited the fire in the study. When she stuck her head in the door, her mother sat on the hearth, ripping up a pair of jeans and holding the pieces between the logs to burn.

As soon as her mother noticed Marsha standing in the room, with a swift move, she grabbed the blood-stained, button-down blouse and stuffed it in between the logs and shoved it deep into the fire with the poker.

Betsy and Julia came in to tell their mother goodnight.

"Marsha," Betsy said. "We're going to watch a movie in Julia's room, do you want to join us?"

The girls went upstairs and left Laura in the study.

As they reached Marsha's bedroom, she motioned for Julia and Betsy to come into her room.

"I didn't want to bring this up in front of Mom tonight, Betsy. But have you and Hal worked through your problems?"

Betsy sat down on the bed and said, "Mom gave me some brilliant advice about not moving out. When Hal first found out I was seeing Jack, he told me to get my stuff out by the time he returned home from work. Besides, I didn't have any place to go. So, I called Mom," Betsy smiled. "She told me to turn my car around and go back home."

"Are you serious?" Julia asked. "Mom and Dad have always told us if we ever needed to come back home to stay for a short stint, that their doors would always be open."

"I know, right? Mom was totally cool about it. She made a valid point, telling me it was my responsibility to keep my family together. As much as I enjoy arguing with her, I knew that was very sound advice."

Betsy's eyes sparkled as she continued.

"So, here I was, making a U-turn on the Interstate. It was an uncongested area, but I turned my car around and followed my mama's advice."

Marsha put her arms around her and said, "Congratulations, I believe you have finally grown up, Betsy. Remember, Mom always has your best interest at heart."

She closed her bedroom door and said, "Speaking of Mom, did either of you notice how shaky she was tonight?"

Marsha rubbed her neck as she sat down on the bed. Then, she told them what she'd discovered about her mother since arriving around three o'clock. Neither of them detected the abrasions on her face or the marks on her wrists. But they did notice she was combing her bangs differently in front and saw her shaky hands.

"I wonder why she keeps suggesting we delay riding. She knows how much those horses meant to us growing up. I don't know about you, but that's why I came home this weekend." Betsy said.

"Do you think she got rid of the horses before the farm sold?" Julia asked. "If so, she might not want us to know about it."

"That's a thought. I'm concerned that Mom's drinking too much," Marsha said. "Losing your husband can't be easy at any age. However, it isn't like her to drink the hard stuff."

"I agree," Betsy said. "Maybe, we should talk to the guy who cares for the horses and find out if he has noticed anything different about Mom. He might know if there was a problem."

"There's no way to be sure," Julia said. "But I'd bet Mom had an accident while out riding and didn't want us to find out."

Betsy got up and started for the door. "I've got an idea, why don't we go down to the stables first thing in the morning before Mom gets up."

Marsha looked at Julia and raised her eyebrows. "Okay. That's a great idea. Let's do it."

Chapter Thirty

Marsha woke early and lay in bed, thinking about the events of the previous day. She couldn't shake the thoughts that her mother's health could be in decline. After losing her dad and being the oldest child, Marsha felt protective of her mother. She couldn't bear to think about losing her to a debilitating mental disease for which there was no known cure.

She threw back the covers from her bed.

Shake it off, Marsha. Mom doesn't have a debilitating mental disease. Worst-case scenario, she fell in the stable and is too embarrassed to tell anyone.

Marsha reached for her phone. <It's 9:30 - time to get up. Get dressed quietly and meet me in the garage in ten minutes>

Marsha finished dressing and made up her bed. Then, she closed the door to her bedroom and slipped downstairs.

Julia was not far behind her. Betsy poured each of them a cup of coffee to enjoy on the ride to the stable.

"Voila! Mom must have gotten up early and made coffee. But don't worry. We left her a cup or two for later."

"Betsy," Marsha said. "You are the best, sista." She used the endearment they often used growing up.

"Thank you."

Betsy and Julia helped Marsha push the Gator out of the garage, for fear their mother would hear the motorized vehicle. As soon as they got onto the driveway, they piled in, and Marsha knocked it out of gear and let it roll. As they entered the curve, they almost ran into a black Mercedes. Marsha swerved and missed it. She gave the Gator some gas, laughing at the thought of skipping out on the meeting with their dad's financial advisor.

They rode in silence while going down the graveled road.

"You know we'll be in deep water when Mom realizes we're gone," Betsy said.

Marsha turned and looked at her, "How do you mean?"

"That Mercedes was probably Dad's financial planner. You know the guy that called last night and asked to meet with us this morning to discuss the family fortune." Betsy said with a chuckle.

Marsha turned to Julia and said, "You're right, of course. Well, we'll head back in a few moments."

"I don't know if we will or not," Julia said. "Looks like something is going on at the barn?"

"It looks to me like someone left the overhead door open," Marsha said.

The white cab of an eighteen-wheeler was visible from the barn's front as they rounded the bend.

"Marsha," Betsy said. "Maybe we should call Mom. This has a bad feel to it. Besides, we need to let her know we'll be heading back in a few minutes."

A short, well-built man, wearing jeans and a black leather jacket emerged from behind the building. He stopped when he saw the all-terrain utility vehicle approaching from a hundred yards away. Then he reached for a walkie-talkie and calmly held it close to his mouth.

Four similarly dressed men moved toward the Gator.

Marsha stopped the Gator and parked a hundred or so yards from the barn. It was difficult to tell what was going on inside from where they sat on the hill. But the girls knew one thing for sure, they had never seen a tractor-trailer backed into the barn before. Something was amiss.

"You better hide that cell phone, Julia," Marsha said.

Suddenly, four angry-looking men surrounded the Gator.

"Perhaps you're right, Betsy," Marsha said as she turned to her sisters. "We should probably turn around and go back to the house and let Mom know what we found. I've never seen that man before. Mom would have told us if she hired someone new."

****

Julia screamed as one man placed a towel around her mouth and pulled her from the vehicle. Another man grabbed Marsha's hair with one hand and around the waist with his other and dragged her onto the ground. A third man slapped his hand over Betsy's mouth, and when she bit him, he knocked her down with a blow to her cheek and then picked her up and threw her over his shoulder. Betsy beat the man's back with her fists and kicked his stomach with her feet, all the while yelling obscenities to him.

They zip-tied and gagged Marsha and Betsy. Only then did Betsy cease her yelling.

The fourth man appeared and motioned them to walk single file behind him. When they began the descent toward the barn, Julia broke away and ran. The taller man ran after her. The movements of his long legs were sprint-like until he caught Julia and wrestled her to the ground. As he forced her on her back, she yanked the towel from her mouth. Then he sat on her thighs as he repeatedly struck her face. Julia panicked and screamed, so he made a fist and bashed her across the bridge of her nose.

"Shut up, bitch," he said with a thick Spanish accent.

The intense pain felt like a lightning bolt flashing through her head, and everything went black. When she regained consciousness, he was standing over her. There was pressure in her head, and her sinuses felt like they were about to explode. It didn't help that her eyes were swollen and watered, but the scary thing was the sight of the blood pouring from her nose and the metallic taste trickling down the back of her throat. Julia knew if she didn't move her head soon, she could drown in her own blood.

He spoke to her in broken English as he reached down to grab her arm. She bounced on her side. He missed and instead grabbed the back of her blouse with such force it ripped, which caused him to stumble on the ground.

The group's leader came out of the barn and issued a harsh order in Spanish and motioned for them to go.

Quickly, he stood up and extended a hand to Julia and said, "Do as I say, if you want to live."

Julia nodded. When she got into the barn, she looked around for her sisters, but they were not visible. Suddenly, she heard a familiar voice. Her head was pounding, and the impact of the blow to her nose was still fresh.

She heard the voice again, and when she looked to the back of the barn, she saw the silhouettes of two men. One man wore a baseball cap, he was of medium height and build. Although she could not see his face, the voice sounded familiar. But she could not remember where she had heard the voice.

The man in charge of Julia shoved her up the back steps of the trailer. As she stepped inside, she turned back and tried to identify the men standing in the far corner of the barn. A moment before they blindfolded her, her eyes locked with the man in the baseball cap, and she could tell from his facial expression that he was shocked by what he saw.

Julia looked down at her opened blouse. The assault caused fresh blood to splatter across the front of her white camisole.

When Julia looked back, he was no longer there. She wondered if he, too, was being held by these savages.

They pushed her hard inside the trailer, and as Julia sat on the floor, she managed to remove the blindfold that slid down around her neck. She saw Marsha and Betsy seated on either side with their legs zip-tied together.

There were pallets of shrink-wrapped squares wrapped in brown paper, and the pungent odor told her the contents were marijuana. Judging from the number of pallets, she estimated there were millions of dollars' worth of drugs within close proximity to her and her sisters.

She wondered if the pallets had been stored inside the barn. Or were they being delivered when she and her sisters arrived on the Gator and interrupted the operation?

As the back door closed, it became pitch black inside the trailer. No one said any more to the girls once they were inside, and they did not understand what was happening to them.

Julia thought about Fitz. He promised that he would be at the farm in time for dinner. If she could just reach her phone in her riding boot, she would text Fitz and he would save them. However, those thoughts soon vanished when she realized that getting a phone signal in the metal trailer was slim to none.

The silence in the trailer was deafening. Julia jumped when the truck's engine started. She realized their captors were leaving, and they were being forced to go with them. Fear flooded her thoughts; they were being kidnapped!

The truck pulled from the barn, and she knew when they reached the road in front of the barn because there was a steep incline which caused a bumpy ride. Julia imagined going by the driveway, which led up to their house. Tears formed in her eyes as she pictured her mother standing in the dining-room window watching as the truck sped down the farm road, unaware of who or what was inside.

Goodbye, Mom. I love you, she said to herself as she dropped her head in anguish.

Chapter Thirty-One

L aura awakened around eight o'clock and went into the kitchen to start the coffee. She noticed the quietness of the house and thought it would be a nice gesture to let the girls sleep late. Another hour would allow more time to apply her makeup and prepare to meet with Rhett and the girls.

For some reason Henry never included her in the meetings with his financial planner. And she wasn't sure what to make of Rhett coming to her house to discuss Henry's portfolio.

They never invited Rhett to their annual New Year's Eve party or the weenie roast and hayride they hosted each fall. Laura and Henry sent over 500 Christmas cards each year, and Henry never added Rhett's name to that list, either.

Now that Henry was gone, Laura found many things hard to understand about the way her husband conducted his affairs. Since Henry handled their finances, Laura had little understanding of their financial position. Still, she created herself a household budget using a spreadsheet she found on the internet. The spreadsheet allowed her to keep up with the monthly bills and the due dates of each payment.

She looked into the mirror, and as she took a sip of coffee, she lifted her bangs, which hung over the right eye and revealed the bruise. The dried blood that seeped from the wound was black, and the discolored skin surrounding the area was sore.

When she stepped out of the shower, she felt immediate relief as she held the warm rag to the abrasion. She applied antiseptic cream and waited for the cream to dry before applying makeup.

As Laura finished dressing, she looked in the mirror and smiled as she applied a pink-colored lipstick. A spark of excitement rushed through her body, a feeling that she thought had died inside her many years ago.

There was confidence in Laura as she returned to the kitchen to refill her coffee while waiting for the girls to come downstairs. When the doorbell rang, she yelled upstairs for the girls to come down for the meeting. Then she walked into the foyer and saw Rhett's black Mercedes parked in the circular drive. Her pulse quickened.

When she opened the door, Rhett gently touched her elbow and brushed her cheek. Laura was unprepared for that gesture. While they walked into the kitchen, she suppressed a smile at his show of affection.

"Would you like some coffee while we wait for the girls to come down?" Laura said.

Rhett laughed.

"What is it?" Laura asked.

"As I pulled in the drive twenty minutes ago, I met a Gator with three beautiful women flying around the curve. It looks like they may have found a quick escape to avoid meeting me."

"Are you serious, Rhett?" Laura said.

"Yes. Perhaps the girls are trying to get a quick ride in before our meeting starts. I wasn't sure how long it would take to drive out here, so I was a few minutes early."

"No, no, no, this isn't happening!" Laura whispered.

"What is it?" Rhett asked.

Laura lifted a finger to her lips when she realized the girls went down to the barn. She reached for a Kleenex and turned away from Rhett when she lost her balance. Fortunately, Rhett leaned forward and caught her. Then he wrapped her in his arms.

She broke free from his grasp.

"I just know something has gone wrong," Laura whispered as she headed out of the kitchen.

Rhett was quick to follow. "Laura, where are you going?"

"I'm going upstairs," she said, "to check their rooms."

"Okay. I'm going with you. You're too upset to be alone," Rhett followed her up the stairs.

When Laura opened the door to Marsha's room, she found the bed was neatly made, and her house shoes were on the floor in front of the nightstand next to her bed. Then, she walked on to Julia's, where she found the same. But when she got back to Betsy's room, the bed was a mess. And Betsy's clothes were strung out over the floor. The blouse Betsy wore the previous day hung across the chair in the corner.

Laura turned to Rhett, who was watching closely from a few feet behind. She hoped he hadn't noticed her panic as she ran her fingers through her hair. But she could not contain her fear.

"What happened to your head?"

"Oh, it's nothing. I just fell, that's all," Laura answered.

Rhett reached for her bangs.

"May I?"

"Yes, of course. But I'm fine."

A few tears escaped her eyes while Rhett inspected the cut on her forehead. As he held her head with his hands, he gently wiped her tears with his thumbs.

When she looked into his eyes, she saw the most adoring expression she ever saw staring back at her. Although they knew very little about each other, she saw in Rhett a fleeting glimpse of something she'd longed for an awfully long time.

Their short gaze ended when they heard the sound of a vehicle coming up the graveled road from the farm.

She gasped. "Oh, my girls!"

Laura jerked away just in time to see a white eighteen-wheeler pass in front of the house as they stood frozen in her daughter's room.

"What's that truck doing down here?" He asked. "Isn't this a dead end road?"

Sobbing, Laura turned and rushed out the door.

Rhett followed.

When they got back downstairs, Laura reached for a pad and jotted something down.

Rhett read the note and pointed to the area above her eye.

She nodded.

"Why don't we run into town and pick up some sandwiches for lunch," Rhett said. "Perhaps when we return, the girls will be back and ready for the meeting."

Laura nodded and placed her finger over her lips.

Chapter Thirty-Two

Laura grabbed her pocketbook and the notepad as they left the house. On the way into town, she continued to write notes explaining the events of the previous day. As Rhett read the notes, he popped in a CD to eliminate the background noise.

"We sure have enjoyed some nice weather this week," Rhett said. "The afternoon temperatures have been unseasonably warm."

He hoped whoever was listening to the device would think it was a typical conversation between Laura and her financial advisor.

When they got into town they found the late morning traffic was light.

"We need to turn at the next traffic light," Rhett said.

But when they stopped in front of the police department, Laura became agitated. With a swift stroke of her pen, she noted the device tracked her whereabouts as well as her voice.

He nodded and turned the vehicle toward his office, which was two blocks away. When he pulled in his office parking lot, Rhett reached for the pad and wrote that he needed to call a friend.

"Do you mind if we stop by my office for a second? I forgot to get a printout before I left this morning," Rhett asked.

"No problem," Laura said, trying to sound casual. "I'll wait in the car."

Rhett grabbed his phone as he stepped outside the car. In less than a minute, he sent off a text message to a detective friend to come to his office. He looked inside the vehicle and gave Laura a thumbs up, showing he was successful in reaching the detective. She nodded as she dabbed her eyes with a Kleenex.

As soon as the detective got there, Rhett filled him in on the situation.

The detective walked over to the car and motioned for Laura to lower her window.

Laura looked up at the detective and mouthed, "Can you help us?" And then she broke down.

He nodded and mouthed, "Yes, ma'am," as he pointed to her ear.

Laura reached and moved her hair back so he would have easy access to the device. As he studied the earring, he was careful not to disturb the apparatus. The detective smiled and patted her shoulder when he completed the examination.

He reached for the notepad and wrote, "Ma'am, I'm detective Troy Wilson. Can I get your home address?"

Laura scribbled the address, and he tore off the piece of paper and handed the pad back to her.

****

Then he motioned to Rhett to come inside with him.

The detective directed the SWAT (special weapons and tactics) team to the farm. When he turned to Rhett, he said. "We will send several guys in a tank truck, but another team will arrive by helicopter in a few moments to find the girls. It's just for added protection. But, considering the way they roughed up Mrs. Whelchel, we can't afford to take any chances with these guys."

"How about the device?" Rhett asked.

"The device can track the movement and voice of Mrs. Whelchel. I'm not sure if this model can capture someone's voice, not in direct contact with it, though. Until we are sure, you should continue to use the notepad to communicate," said the detective.

"Is there anyone in the department that would know about this particular device?"

"I'll make a call to a colleague and find out. Just give me a few moments. While I'm making the call, why don't you slip a note to Mrs. Whelchel about the SWAT team? She's pretty upset."

"Yes, she is, and rightfully so. She's lost her husband, and now she suspects her daughters are in danger," Rhett said.

"Do you mind if I ask you a question?" Detective Wilson said while he placed a call to his colleague.

"Sure," Rhett answered.

"What is your relationship to the Whelchel family?" Detective Wilson asked.

Rhett smiled, knowing where the detective was going with the line of questioning.

"I was Mr. Whelchel's financial advisor. Laura and I scheduled a meeting at her house this morning to review his finances. Her girls are here for the weekend, and she asked them to attend the meeting. That is how I became involved in this situation. It was a random occurrence."

"It's a good thing you were there. Imagine what would've happened if you hadn't been there?" Wilson responded.

"They might not have slipped off to the barn had we not scheduled the meeting."

"Well, I'm sure they would have slipped off at some point. Mrs. Whelchel couldn't take a chance on telling them what happened to her at the barn. Although I'm surprised, one of her daughters didn't noticed that cut over her eye. It looks rather nasty. Perhaps I should ask a member of the EMT to come over and check it out."

Laura sat in the car, wondering what was taking place inside when Rhett brought a note out to her. The mention of the SWAT team scared her as she fought to hold herself together.

She reached for the pad and began to scribble.

"Is the detective expecting them to communicate with the men who did this to me?" She said as she pointed to her right eye.

He explained that they were more interested in getting the girls away from the farm, but at some point, they would go after the men, too.

Rhett knew that with hostage situations, it was reasonable to expect demands for sizable sums of ransom money. Then again, he dared not mention that to Laura now. It amazed him at how strong she was, given the potential danger of the situation. Naturally, she cried a great deal, and what parent wouldn't be upset. Considering that she'd maintained any level of calm throughout the morning was a miracle. As he stood outside the car, he asked if she was hungry or would like a coffee or bottled water.

Rhett read the note, "Diet Coke." He nodded.

As Rhett walked back inside, the detective followed him into the break room and said, "We have just received a report from the SWAT team."

Rhett's eyes widened as he asked, "And?"

"When the SWAT team arrived, the barn was empty except for a few items of equipment. They checked the stable and the horses appear to be unharmed."

"How about the girls?" Rhett asked.

"They didn't find them. However, the SWAT team found a bracelet on the floor of the barn. He's sending over a picture for Mrs. Whelchel to identify."

"Well, what does that mean?" Rhett asked. "Did the girls return to the house, or not?"

"No. The detectives found the Gator a few hundred feet from the barn, and there's no one in the house. Apparently, Mrs. Whelchel left the front door unlocked, and they searched the inside of the house, too."

The detective paused and looked at his phone.

"Here's a picture of the bracelet, we need Mrs. Whelchel to identify it for the SWAT team."

Rhett looked at the phone as he slowly walked outside to the car.

Chapter Thirty-Three

L aura immediately recognized the bracelet as belonging to Betsy. One that she suspected Betsy had received as a gift from the personal trainer. She laid down on the front seat and sobbed.

Laura continued to lay on the front seat, thinking about their predicament. She jumped at the sound of her cell phone, and when she saw that it was Andrew, she quickly wiped her nose and answered.

Andrew mentioned a recent development and asked if she could meet at his office. He explained that he received a call from a person whose name was not available and asked for a Facetime meeting at twelve o'clock.

She tried to speak in a normal tone, but she had cried so much her voice was hoarse. "I'm on my way to lunch with Rhett Louis, but I'll ask him to drop me off at your office in time for the meeting."

When they got close to Andrew's office, Rhett pulled into a convenience store, and when he finished pumping the gas, he pulled the vehicle over to the side of the store. He reached for the pad and scribbled at note. He explained that he would walk over to Andrew's office to let him know what was going on and asked her to go into the store, get a few snacks, and pay for the gas.

Rhett's note also asked her to tell the owner Rhett planned to leave his car in the parking lot for a few minutes.

Laura picked up the money and the car keys and went into the store. Remembering her comments were being monitored, she slipped a note to the owner. As he accepted the paper, he looked into her eyes and smiled, as if he knew there was an immediate problem.

She said, "I got hungry and thought I'd pick up a couple of hot dogs and go out to the river for a picnic."

The owner acted as if he understood her situation, and then commented that the weather was perfect for a lunch at the lake. When the owner gave Laura the change and receipt, he squeezed her hand and said, "Bless you."

Laura left the store and walked down the street to Andrew's office. Rhett met her in the reception area and handed her a note about the recent development. He reached behind her ear and pushed the on/off switch on the earring.

They went into Andrew's office and sat on the sofa as they discussed what they found at the farm.

Laura was nervous that Rhett had cut off the device, and she wrote him a note.

He reached for her hand and said, "Don't worry. The detective said it was okay to cut it off since it was apparent the men had left the farm. Although, if you prefer, we will turn it back on in a few minutes. Laura, we need to talk openly with you about the girls," as he patted her hand.

"Okay. We'll leave it off for a few minutes."

Drew Byrd, Andrew's son, and partner walked into the office and held up a piece of paper for his dad.

"What's that, son?" Andrew asked.

"I found this message on the fax machine, it's dated today." Drew placed the fax on his father's desk.

Andrew read aloud the demand for one million dollars in unmarked bills in exchange for Henry Whelchel's daughters. When he finished reading the demand, he looked over at Laura and noticed she had fainted and had slumped over onto Rhett.

Laura stirred as she remembered Andrew reading the demand for one million dollars.

What would Henry do if he were alive? I'm sure he would know how to deal with these people. Before she finished her train of thought, she passed out.

Chapter Thirty-Four

When the tractor-trailer stopped several hours later, a hidden door opened from the cab, and one of the men came into the trailer and tied a rag around each of the girl's eyes. Their captor removed the zip-ties from their legs, handcuffed them to each other, and led them in a single file to a second trailer parked nearby.

He was gentle as he helped each of them into the back of the trailer. The smell of human waste was horrific, and he apologized about the conditions. Eventually, he removed the blindfold from their eyes. They saw perhaps a hundred girls and young women, all of whom appeared to be drugged. Marsha noticed a Hispanic girl sitting near them. She had gorgeous skin and extensions in her hair, but she never made eye contact with anyone. The girl wore stylish clothes, much like the college-age students, Marsha taught at the university.

Then the door closed, and the trailer went dark.

Marsha and her sisters watched a documentary about sex trafficking on 60 Minutes one weekend while they were at their mother's house. She recognized a few signs as she watched the young girls.

Marsha was sitting between Julia and Betsy, and the touch of her sisters' hand comforted her.

Julia used her index finger and spelled out SEX TRAFFICKING into Marsha's hand.

Marsha elbowed her two times. Julia assumed her answer was yes. Then, Julia spelled out BETSY CRYING, and Marsha elbowed one time, as in no. And, with those two questions, they established their method of communication.

Boredom set in as the hours passed. The humming of the tires moving down the highway worked like a sedative. Before long, it lulled the girls to sleep.

Suddenly, the truck came to an abrupt stop, and the engine shut off. After a length of time, a door from the cab opened, which allowed light to filter into the trailer.

After a few moments when Marsha's eyes had adjusted to the sunlight, she focused her attention on the various ages of the girls. One beautiful Hispanic girl, who could not have been over twelve or thirteen years old, was sleeping near them, and her innocence grabbed at Marsha's heart. There were girls of all ages and ethnicity. Some were well dressed, while others appeared to be partially clothed. Two of the captors stepped into the trailer, each carrying a large black bag.

The smell of food mixed with the stench of human waste was nauseating. They watched as the men handed each person a hamburger wrapped in white paper and a water bottle.

Marsha opened her water bottle and placed it between her knees. She helped Betsy get her bottle opened and insisted she ate the hamburger. Then she did the same for Julia. While her sisters ate, Marsha watched the other girls sleep while their food and water went untouched. She was thankful that she and her sisters escaped being drugged and were still alive.

What would Dad have us do in a situation like this? He was such a wise man, and perhaps he understood the criminal mindset better than anyone because of his line of work. First, Dad would tell us to keep a clear head and not do anything stupid. He always had such a calming nature during times of crisis.

After the break, and as they resumed their journey, Marsha closed her eyes and thought of her father.

Once again, Marsha was in her teens, perhaps fifteen years old, sitting in the alcove next to her dad's office. She had listened to her father's conversation with a man accused of stealing a gun from his brother-in-law over the Fourth of July weekend. When the meeting ended, there was a buzz from the phone on the desk, and she heard her father say, "I thought the meeting was tomorrow afternoon."

A silence.

"Okay. Then send him in. But hold my calls, I need a few minutes to talk with this man."

Marsha sat and listened to the man who she learned was Thomas Kirkpatrick, a sales agent with Mutual of Omaha Insurance Company. He explained that the company had issued the million-dollar life insurance policy he had requested. The beneficiary was Sofia Suarez Romano, and the contingent beneficiary was his estate, just as Henry had suggested. While her Dad and Mr. Kirkpatrick discussed the policy, Marsha learned they would deduct the premiums from his payroll check. A fact her father wanted to keep secret.

Her dad's last comment before Mr. Kirkpatrick left was, "Remember, my wife can never find out about this, Thomas."

When the agent left, Marsha waited a few minutes and walked into her father's office. It was evident Henry had forgotten his daughter was in the next room studying, because the insurance policy remained on the top of his desk.

"Dad, I'm thirsty, can I get a soft drink from the break room, please?"

"Yes. Of course, dear." He waved her off as he continued to look at the policy.

When Marsha returned, her father continued to read the document while Marsha stood in front of his desk.

"Daddy?"

"Yes, sweetheart."

"Daddy, I need to ask you something."

"Okay, dear. Give me just a second longer."

He stopped reading and neatly folded the policy. "Okay, sweetheart. You've been so quiet I forgot you were in the next room."

He looked over at Marsha and smiled, "Do you need me to read over that paper you've been working on this afternoon?"

"No, sir. I just want to know, who is Sofia Romano?"

Henry looked at the policy on his desk.

"Why isn't Mom the beneficiary of that policy? Wouldn't she need the money if you died?"

"Marsha, I can appreciate your concern, but this was a complicated situation." He explained that although he loved his daughters more than anything else in the world, two people sometimes marry and remain married for odd reasons.

"Does that mean, you didn't love Mom when you married?"

"Of course not, sweetheart. I love your mom for a variety of reasons. First, she is an excellent mother to you, girls. She's also smart and beautiful, and she's made a lovely home for us to enjoy. You'll agree that your mom is a superb cook, and she throws the best parties in town. I want you to know that marrying your mother was the right decision for me."

"Well, what does that mean exactly, Dad? It sounds to me like you wanted to pick someone else, is that what you are saying?"

"No, no. Not at all, dear. I just feel like I made the right choice when I married your mom."

Marsha sat down in the chair in front of his desk. Without realizing she was watching his every move, Henry picked up the policy and rubbed his finger across the name of Sofia Suarez Romano.

"Dad, is Mom the love of your life, or did you love Ms. Romano?"

"Yes, I did. I mean..." Henry closed his eyes and shook his head at the carelessness of the remark. "I knew Ms. Romano, but..."

"You were in love with her, weren't you?"

Henry got up from behind his desk, walked around and sat in the chair next to Marsha, and said, "Listen, honey, you're a smart girl, but this is a complicated situation. Although, I have never lied to you or to either of your sisters. There are things in my life, and perhaps even your mother's life, about which you need not know."

"Well, okay, Dad. Just tell me you loved Mom more than Ms. Romano. Please tell me that my Mom is the love of your life."

Henry rubbed his eyes and looked at Marsha, "This is all you need to know about this situation, honey. Once I explain this, we will never discuss this subject again. Do you understand?"

Tears welled up in Marsha's eyes, as she nodded.

"I love your mother very much. Although, I'm not sure what you mean when you say the love of my life. However, your mom and you girls are the most important people in my world."

He stood and walked over and leaned against the windowsill. "Marsha, you will find that we often make decisions in life based on what is in our best interest. And my decision to marry your mother was the absolute best decision I could have ever made for my career and my family."

As her father walked back to his desk with tears in his eyes, he said, "Always remember, you and your sisters are the best things that have ever happened to me."

Chapter Thirty-Five

A ndrew looked at Rhett and asked, "Are you sure she's okay?"
"Yes, Andrew. She's breathing. The poor lady is exhausted," Rhett replied. "She slept very little last night, and it's evident this shocking news just caused her to faint."

Rhett turned his attention back to Laura and patted her face while he spoke to her in a gentle, soothing voice. "Wake up now, Laura, and take a sip of water for me." Finally, she opened her eyes, and her body felt like a dishrag in his arms.

"Okay," Laura said.

Rhett continued to work with her for a few minutes longer and convinced her to take a bite of the hotdog she had purchased at the convenience store. He offered the other one to Andrew, but he declined. So, he ate it himself and coaxed Laura to take another bite until she had eaten most of it.

Andrew said, "I can get Drew to run out for sandwiches if you like. Or perhaps Laura would prefer a nice bowl of soup."

Laura nodded her head as she took a sip of water and said, "Thank you, Andrew. I'm fine. Would you please reread the demand?"

Andrew reached for the paper and slowly read it aloud.

Laura turned to Rhett and cried, "How can I get together one million dollars before eight o'clock tonight? That's impossible!"

Andrew looked at Rhett, "It's almost noon. I'm sure we'll find out more information during the meeting."

He called his son, Drew, into his office and asked him to prepare the overhead screen behind the conference table for the Facetime Meeting.

Laura held her head in her hands and looked up and said, "Perhaps I should contact Betsy's husband, Hal, and Julia's friend, Fitz."

Startled, Andrew said, "No, Laura. We can't involve either of them right now. To do so could compromise the safety of your girls."

Laura looked shocked.

Rhett reached for her hands, "He's right, Laura. We've got to maintain a clear head and not do anything that would jeopardize their safety. The fewer people we involve at this point, the better."

"Of course. You both are right," Laura said. "I'm afraid something will happen to them. No. I can't even think that!"

At twelve o'clock, just as promised, a man appeared on the screen. He wore a dark blue, three-piece suit, and he sat in a high back leather chair in front of a bookshelf. It appeared to be an office of any ordinary attorney. As they watched the screen, Rhett knew they were not dealing with an attorney. There was something in the manner of his speech, which showed a lack of formal education. The words he chose were not indicative of someone who had undergone extensive training of legal issues.

Laura's body felt rigid, as Rhett reached for her hand.

The man on the screen was stoic, but very animated in his speech.

"I have on competent authority that the girls are well and currently headed for the US border. They should arrive in New Orleans at around five o'clock. If the funds are ready on time, they will remain unharmed and dropped off at a French Quarter hotel. If not, they will continue their journey. They should arrive in Houston at eleven o'clock."

He continued to explain from there, they would head to the US border. If the funds were not available before they reached their destination, Laura's daughters would be sold into a sex trafficking operation.

Andrew waited for him to finish his explanation, and said, "So your people are not involved in the sex trafficking business, is that correct?"

He did not acknowledge the question. It was apparent by everyone in the room, the answer to that question was not in his script.

Rhett looked at his watch and realized it would be a challenge to meet the demand by five o'clock, if they could get the money together at all.

Then, Andrew cleared his voice and said, "Thank you. Is there anything more my client should know?"

There was dead silence as the screen went blank. It was clear the call was over.

When the call ended, Rhett noticed he was still holding onto Laura's hand. He felt a tenderness toward Laura that he had not experienced toward anyone since his wife's illness and subsequent death. Although it had been over thirty years, Rhett could still see the lighting in the ICU area, and the smell of death that permeated the room when his wife died. Rhett had managed to suppress the pain from her loss for many years, which was the only way he had survived after her death.

As Andrew got up from the conference table and went back to his desk, Rhett lifted Laura's hand to his cheek. Laura looked at Rhett as their eyes locked for several seconds.

Chapter Thirty-Six

R hett's mind flashed back to the day in April 1977, when his wife, Suzanne, called his office to tell him she was experiencing a terrible headache.

Usually, he was particularly attentive to the requests of his young bride. After all, it was her first pregnancy, and she remained in a constant state of angst since finding out she was pregnant. However, he was preparing to meet with an important client. It was a young lawyer, who had recently tried a high-profile case, and had won a huge settlement. The case had attracted state and national attention relating to a wrongful death case involving a senator from the state of Georgia.

Rhett thought about the cavalier reaction to his wife's call, and once again, felt the regret that he had dismissed her pain without trying to help her. The memory of that call was etched in his mind.

"Rhett, can you please just take the afternoon off and come home? I feel like something isn't quite right, and I don't want to be here alone."

"Suzanne, I've got an important meeting this afternoon. You know what this client can mean to my business. I can't just cancel a meeting thirty minutes before it's scheduled to start. But I'll try to keep the meeting as short as possible."

"Rhett, listen to me. I feel like the top of my head is about to explode. Will you call Dr. Richardson, and find out if there's anything I can take that won't harm the baby? We don't have any pain medication in the house."

When he hung up from the call, he went into the conference room. As it turned out, his new client was more knowledgeable of stocks and bonds than Rhett realized. The meeting took much longer than expected because he had to stop to answer each question posed to him about the portfolio he had designed for the substantial investment.

Rhett looked at his watch as he returned to his office and saw that it was almost five o'clock. Remembering the discussion with his wife, he quickly picked up the phone. He dialed the number to her OBGYN's office, and after a brief pause, they patched him through to the doctor. He explained to him the excruciating pain that Suzanne had described earlier in the afternoon, He needed to know what to pick up from the pharmacy to help her pain.

The doctor said, "You're still at your office, right?"

"Correct. I've been in a meeting this afternoon. But I'm about to head out."

"Okay. Perhaps, first, you should go home and check on Suzanne's condition. Then give me a call back. Rhett, you may need to bring her in this evening. I'm hesitant to prescribe a pain reliever without an examination."

Rhett stopped by the break room, grabbed a Coke from the refrigerator. He was thirsty because he had spent the afternoon talking to a man whose new fortune could make a big difference in his financial planning business. Still, now Rhett was eager to get home.

As soon as he locked the office and jumped into his car, he pressed his cellphone's home button, to check on Suzanne. There was no answer, and he hung up after about five rings. In an instant he redialed the number as he pulled out into the heavy afternoon traffic - still, no answer.

He panicked when he remembered the conversation they had earlier about her headache.

Why did I dismiss her as I did? She could be really sick.

When Suzanne called the office and needed something, it was normal for Rhett to drop everything and run to the grocery store or go pick up lunch for her. Whatever she needed, he stopped whatever he was doing to handle it. He had always placed her needs before his own.

But not this time.

On the way home from work, he took a shortcut to avoid the afternoon traffic. As he turned into their subdivision, he decided to park in the driveway and go in the side door, instead of raising the garage door and entering through the kitchen as was his routine.

As he pulled into the drive, he noticed the paper still lay in the driveway from the morning delivery. When he walked through the side door, he glanced into the adjacent laundry room. The dirty clothes he had placed on the washing machine earlier in the morning were still in the same place. His heart raced as he yelled out to Suzanne.

"Honey. I'm home. Where are you?"

The house was quiet. He went into the kitchen and took the last sip of his coke and dropped the can in the garbage. The dirty breakfast dishes were still on the table.

"Suzanne! Where are you?" He continued into the family room and then onto the living area.

She didn't answer.

Walking toward the master suite, he saw the unmade bed, but she was not there, either. Frantically, he walked into the adjoining bathroom. When he stepped back into the bedroom, he stopped and rubbed the temples of his head.

Then, he heard a movement and something that sounded like a small groan. He went toward the sound, which was on the other side of the bed. And, there Suzanne lay, passed out on the floor. She was wearing the same cotton gown she had worn to bed the previous night. The sight of her swollen body shocked Rhett, and it was clear she had struggled before she fell.

Fortunately, there were no cuts or abrasions on her body. She whimpered as Rhett gently lifted her onto the bed. Softly, he patted her face as he reassured her that he would take care of her and the baby. Immediately, Rhett reached for the phone and dialed 911 and then called the doctor's office. The phone rang only once, and he knew then that Dr. Richardson had waited around for his call.

In a state of panic, Rhett told the doctor that he had already called 911 and explained how he found Suzanne lying on the floor from an apparent fall. He also explained the swelling that had developed in her extremities.

"I'll meet you in the emergency room in about fifteen to twenty minutes. I'll call ahead and let them know to expect you."

When the ambulance arrived at the hospital, a nurse directed them to a small room in the emergency area. Doctor Richardson came in and took one look at Suzanne and started issuing orders to the attending nurse. After a brief examination, he looked over at Rhett and motioned for him to step outside.

"Rhett, this is serious."

"What do you mean, Doc?"

"Well, the swelling means she has possibly developed preeclampsia, which is a pregnancy complication characterized by high blood pressure and signs of damage to other organ systems, most often the liver and kidneys. The swelling that we are seeing in her extremities indicates her kidneys are already compromised. I have ordered a battery of tests, and as soon as I receive the results, we'll talk again."

"When I left this morning, she was fine," Rhett said. "Of course, she's been gaining some weight, but she's pregnant. It's common for pregnant women to gain weight, right?"

"Let's try to remain calm, Rhett. These complications often sneak upon us. Her blood pressure was a little high last week during her checkup. But it wasn't anything out of the norm for a woman of twenty-six weeks."

During the early morning hours, after Dr. Richardson reviewed the test results, he met with Rhett again. He explained they were trying to get the swelling under control, but they would need to take the baby if they were unsuccessful.

The next morning Dr. Richardson stopped and checked Suzanne while completing his rounds. Then he motioned for Rhett to walk outside the unit. He explained the tests had found excessive protein in her urine. Since arriving at the hospital, the output had decreased substantially. The blood work showed reduced levels of platelets, and she had also developed impaired liver function. They discovered fluid in her lungs, which was causing shortness of breath.

"The test results tell us that the likely reason for her unconscious state, when you found her on the floor, was because of a seizure. It's common in patients with eclampsia, essentially preeclampsia plus seizures."

"What could have caused this preeclampsia?" Rhett asked with tears in his eyes.

Dr. Richardson placed his hand on his back and said, "The experts are not exactly sure, but the basic theory is we believe the problem begins in the placenta, the organ that nourishes the fetus throughout the pregnancy. Early in the pregnancy, new blood vessels develop to send blood to the placenta. In Suzanne's case, the new blood vessels are not functioning properly." He paused for Rhett to process the information.

Rhett slumped down in a nearby chair, placed his elbows on his knees, and covered his face with his hands. He quickly understood this had become a life or death situation for both Suzanne and their unborn baby.

"We're doing everything we know to help her get through this. But we need to deliver the baby, or else they both could die."

When Rhett got himself together, he and Dr. Richardson went back into the unit to talk with Suzanne. She was almost delirious from the pain from her head's frontal area, which he learned later was caused by a cerebral hemorrhage. Suzanne reached for Dr. Richardson's arm. And in a pitiful and desperate plea, "If you must choose between the baby or me, please save my baby? Promise me, Dr. Richardson, that you'll do that for me."

Then Suzanne turned to Rhett and placed her hand on the side of his face. "Rhett, promise me, please?"

Rhett placed his hand over hers and clung to it, while realizing his wife was making the ultimate sacrifice.

"Promise me, Rhett!"

Rhett lowered his head to avoid her seeing the tears in his eyes. He then moved her hand to his lips and softly kissed her fingers, as he mouthed okay.

Chapter Thirty-Seven

Marsha heard a woman's voice approach them in the trailer's corner where they sat since their arrival. The authoritative tone of the woman speaking identified her as the "Bottom." The Bottom Bitch, was the word she remembered from the documentary, defined as a person given authority to manage and control the movement of the victims. Marsha noticed the Bottom, in this case, was no more than thirty years old. Although, it was hard to determine an exact age because she had a stocky build, and wore her hair cut close to the scalp. Otherwise, one could quickly distinguish her position by the many keys on the massive silver chain attached to her belt loop, that hung down the side of her pants leg.

The woman shined a flashlight on the faces of Marsha, Julia, and Betsy, "You girls are not with the rest of the group, are you?"

Marsha nodded as her eyes settled on the serpent figure tattooed on her right wrist. She recognized the symbol as a brand of the organization featured from the documentary they watched on sex trafficking.

"Well, you better be out of here by the time we reach New Orleans. Because I need this space for the next pickup."

Then she cut off the flashlight and moved away from them.

As she stopped a few feet away, Marsha heard her say, "You girls are moving out at the next stop, so be ready to get out."

Chapter Thirty-Eight

A ndrew let out a deep breath and said, "Okay. We've got to get moving. Time is of the essence."

Laura looked at Rhett and then to Andrew and said, "I don't know where I can get that kind of money."

Rhett said, "You may not have to. I'm texting Detective Wilson now. They have resources within their undercover division that can assist with these types of issues. Let's hope the person on the screen was truthful with his information. Then we must wait and find out what the detective suggests."

Andrew looked at his watch, and it occurred to him they would deposit the funds from the sale of the farm into Laura's account by the end of the day.

"Laura, do you have mobile access to your bank account?"

"Yes, I do," Laura said. "Why do you ask?"

"We're expecting one million dollars in your account by the end of the afternoon. Suppose the money isn't sitting in your account when the bank closes at five o'clock. The sale of the property is officially off, as per the contractual agreement."

Her eyes grew large, "However, if they deposit the money as promised, we can use that money to trade for the girls."

194 · RENEE PROPES

Rhett said, "No. Laura. That would be like giving the farm away. It'd be like handing your money over to a bunch of gangsters. You would be out the money and the farm, with no guarantee you will get the girls back."

Andrew went to check the fax machine, leaving Rhett and Laura alone in his office. Rhett said, "Laura, I'll help you get the money together. I've already started liquidating some funds to use."

Laura smiled.

"I can't let you do that, Rhett. This is my problem, and I know that somehow we will reach an agreement. I don't care if we use the money from the farm's sale for the girls, I'll do it. And, when this is over, I'll sell the house and go rent an apartment." She paused, "or live in Marsha's basement… She's got plenty of room in her house."

Although he was scrolling through his phone, Laura knew he was engaged in the conversation because he continued to make eye contact.

"Or you can move in with me." He said as he looked up from his cell phone, winked at her, and then continued to scroll.

It was a casual remark that surprised Laura and caused her to blush. Then, she grabbed her phone, walked to the window, and accessed her online banking account.

"Rhett, the balance hasn't changed since the last time I checked it earlier in the week."

Rhett turned and glanced at Laura.

She put her head back and looked to the sky and closed her eyes. Although she was silent, her lips moved.

"Laura, we'll work this out and get your girls back safely. Just trust me."

****

When Andrew came back into the office, Laura went back to the sofa and sat next to Rhett.

"Okay. The FBI agent is here," Andrew announced.

Bill Bowen walked several steps behind Andrew into the office, greeted Laura, and introduced himself to Rhett. "Your attorney tells me your daughters are part of a hostage situation."

"Yes. Mr. Bowen. That's correct," Laura said. "Can you help us get the girls back?"

"I'll do my best." He explained the protocol for handling kidnapping cases through the bureau. After he talked for a few moments, he concluded with: "But if the truck makes it to Houston, there's a distinct possibility that you may never see them again."

Then he offered suggestions about how they should proceed.

Andrew looked sideways at the agent and then glanced at Rhett as he raised his eyebrows. Andrew had been busy taking notes on a legal pad, but he stopped writing when Mr. Bowen mentioned Houston. He looked back at Rhett, who apparently, heard the same thing, although it was evident that Laura hadn't caught it.

Out of respect for Agent Bowen's position with the bureau, they allowed him ample time to finish his suggestions before Andrew got up from his desk and thanked him for stopping by. "We'll be in touch as soon as we have more information." Then, he walked him out.

When Andrew returned, Laura asked, "What just happened? Mr. Bowen acted totally different from the time he was at my house."

Rhett said, "Laura, I believe, and I think Andrew will agree, that perhaps Mr. Bowen knows a great deal more about this operation, than he's telling."

"What gave you that idea?"

Andrew explained that no one mentioned the route the captors were taking. "We had not yet disclosed the information we had learned from the Facetime meeting when Mr. Bowen mentioned the Houston stop. How would he know that information without somehow being involved in the operation? Indeed, none of us told him."

Laura said, "I thought the FBI knew everything."

Andrew and Rhett chuckled.

Andrew said, "I'm afraid that's the consensus of most everyone."

"Well, perhaps we should contact Agent Roberts out of the Washington office," Laura said. "He was kind and accommodating when they investigated the loss of their agent. And, he should have a higher level of clearance, too."

The skin on Andrew's forehead wrinkled as he looked over at Rhett.

"Actually, that's a great idea," Andrew said. "I'll ask my assistant to find his number."

Chapter Thirty-Nine

The helicopter carrying Roberts, the Special Agent in Charge from the Washington office of the Federal Bureau of Investigation was flying low as it approached the city of Abington. Roberts instructed the pilot to contact air traffic control for a discreet location to land the helicopter.

"We can't afford to create any media attention," he said. "It would only compromise our mission. Let me know their recommendations before you schedule the landing."

It took less than five minutes for the pilot to complete the request. "Sir, the Air Traffic Control Tower suggests using the helipad at the Medical Center in Abington. They will get permission from the hospital and will guarantee us complete secrecy of the landing."

SAIC Roberts removed two files from his briefcase and reviewed the information involving the agent's body found in the creek at the Whelchel farm.

Then, he opened the second file. He shook his head when he examined the pictures of Mrs. Whelchel's grown daughters.

Each year, we are receiving more and more cases like this. But usually they involve much younger girls.

When he received the Abington call, he asked Andrew Byrd, the Whelchel's attorney, to brief him on everything he knew about the current situation. Anytime a local SWAT team gets involved in a case, they alert the FBI's Washington office. Roberts had instructed the SWAT team to keep the kidnapped information quiet, meaning Washington would handle the case going forward without involvement from the regional office.

As Roberts looked at the billowing clouds outside the chopper window, he thought about the scenario in which the attorney explained the meeting with Agent Bowen. The Bureau had been monitoring Bowen for some time. The previous two operations Bowen commanded, involving the drug cartel, were unsuccessful. However, the kidnapping, which originated from the same property where they found the special agent's body, was too coincidental for him to allow Bowen's involvement.

The drug cartel, which the FBI informants had traced to Colombia, supplied the marijuana and cocaine to the distributor. Here, the drug lord was of Colombian American descent. Roberts had followed this cartel for eighteen-months. Abington was less than a two-hour drive to the world's busiest passenger airport, although one would not expect to find an operation of this magnitude in rural North Georgia. Otherwise, the logistics involved in transporting the drugs by land to a nearby coastal port would be challenging.

The pilot turned to the FBI official and said, "Sir, prepare to land in two minutes."

Agent Roberts looked outside the window of the helicopter and inspected the beautiful landscape of the city. He was close enough to spot the courthouse near the town square. To the east of the downtown area was the large medical center, where they would be landing. Looking at the vehicles traveling the busy streets, he commented to the pilot, "This is America at its finest."

Those people are going about their business, working jobs, raising children, and living life in a small town. Many of them are like the rest of us, and they're looking forward to getting off work. Perhaps they're thinking about what they'll have for dinner tonight. Or wondering how they'll make their mortgage payment this month. Little do they know there is an illegal and dangerous drug operation active in their own backyard.

As promised, there was only one unmarked car sitting near the helipad at the Medical Center to transport Roberts to the law firm, a quick five-minute drive away. As he looked at his watch, it was 1500 hours. It had taken less than two hours for Roberts to make the trip from Washington.

The copilot, a Bureau special agent, reviewed the picture of Andrew Byrd, the attorney waiting in the unmarked vehicle below. As soon as the chopper set down, he jumped out and quickly went over to confirm his identity. He turned back to the pilot and gave a thumbs up. At that point, Agent Roberts exited the chopper. As Roberts closed the car door, the helicopter lifted off and headed south, waiting for further instructions from the Bureau.

Chapter Forty

Encouraged, Marsha squeezed her sisters' hands, sitting to each side of her in the cramped trailer.

New Orleans, she thought. *It would take close to seven hours to travel from Abington to New Orleans in normal traffic conditions. Could the truck be heading to a drop-off point in New Orleans? Perhaps, someone had made a demand for money in exchange for us.*

She had held her bladder throughout the morning. However, when the Bottom shined the flashlight in her face, the fear she experienced caused her bladder to relax. Marsha smelled the strong urine that saturated the seat of her jeans. In any other situation, it would have embarrassed her. Still, she realized she was at the mercy of these people, and her main concern was staying alive.

There was a loud blood-curdling scream, followed by a moaning sound that they heard from the front of the trailer. Her eyes searched the darkness for a sign of light when she saw a figure holding a torch-like instrument. Marsha recognized the smell of burning flesh and realized the operative had just branded another young girl. A hard slap vibrated throughout the trailer, and there was another piercing scream which lasted for a few seconds.

Then, there was a hushed silence in the trailer, as the girls were fearful they would become the next victim of the branding.

There was a shuffling in the trailer's back, which required a lot of movement in the surrounding sections. Marsha followed the flashlight as it approached their area, while the Bottom barked orders along the way.

"Move over to the right of the door, now," said the Bottom. "You're up next."

Marsha and her sisters nodded in agreement as they stood and stared toward the light.

"Remember, move fast when I tell you to get off. We have other problems to handle once you're gone."

Her sisters moved in unison to the area where they would exit at the time of their release. An undercurrent of excitement ran through Marsha's body as she thought about being reunited with her mother. She suppressed the thoughts about being killed or sold at the border, as she tried to remain positive in her thoughts.

Thinking about the many young girls at the university, Marsha decided to introduce a course of study to educate young women to avoid the pitfalls of being taken into a trafficking situation.

There was much to consider, realizing many of her young students came from affluent families.

This trafficking organization crosses all socio-economic borders. These people have no regard for income or race. The only criteria it seemed they preyed upon were perhaps a lack of self-confidence recognized in young girls, from the girl's appearances in the trailer, the younger, the better.

Sitting in the dark trailer, in what she hoped would be for the last few minutes of her captivity, she looked forward to the promised release at the next stop. Marsha looked upwards as she said a silent prayer for God's hand of safety to be upon all the young girls left behind.

Chapter Forty-One

SAIC Roberts sat at the conference table and reviewed the Facetime tape and suppressed his anger at the man's absurdity posing as an attorney. It was apparent the man was an actor and not even a professional one, at that. Perhaps he was someone they had pulled off the street who didn't understand what he was getting himself involved in, but just needed a quick buck.

Reviewing his papers, he noted they dispatched the SWAT team to New Orleans. The helicopter circled the airspace around the city, trying not to alarm the local air traffic tower. Another SWAT chopper remained in Abington and watched for movement on the farm.

The antique clock in Andrew Byrd's office struck sixteen hundred hours. Roberts turned to him and asked, "Excuse me, Andrew. What time do the banks in this area close?"

Looking at his watch, "They remain open until five o'clock, sir."

"Laura," Andrew asked. "Have you checked your online bank account lately?"

She picked up her phone and accessed her account. She saw the transaction showing the deposit in her account. Then her phone rang, it was her personal banker advising her of the deposit.

"Excuse me a moment," she covered the phone with her hand as she asked Rhett, "Should we leave the funds in that account or move it over to my investment account with your firm?"

Roberts turned and said, "Do you have another account at the bank, Mrs. Whelchel?"

"Yes. I have a money market account with the same bank."

"Transfer the funds into that account. Let's not move the funds outside the bank."

Continuing the conversation with the bank representative, Laura asked, "Would you transfer the funds to my money market account before leaving today?" Laura paused and nodded as she listened to the bank representative.

"Thank you, dear. I appreciate you doing that for me. Can you advise me when the transfer is complete?"

When she hung up the phone, Laura accessed her money market account and found she had completed the transfer.

Roberts rose from the conference table and walked over to the chair next to where Laura and Rhett were sitting near Andrew's desk. "The deposit into your account is a good sign, Mrs. Whelchel. It implies, but doesn't completely eliminate the buyers' involvement with the drug cartel. That has been a significant concern since Mr. Byrd made me aware of the land closing scheduled for tomorrow. The wiring of funds to the Seller is perhaps the most critical transaction of the closing. When the wire is complete, there is literally no way the funds can be retrieved. Although I encouraged you to move the funds, had the kidnappers been privy to information regarding the closing, they would continue to track the money after you receive it."

"The timing of that deposit is good news. We now have time to get to the bank and withdraw the money and meet the next deadline." Laura said.

"No, ma'am. We won't be using your money to make the swap. I've got people in place in New Orleans with unmarked bills, with strict instructions that we see your daughters and speak to them before the suitcase is released."

Laura's phone rang. "This is my daughter's boyfriend, Fitz. Should I take the call?"

Roberts said, "No. Let's wait about answering the call. Let's see if he leaves a message."

As soon as her phone showed a voice mail, she handed the phone to Roberts, and he listened to the message.

"Hi, Laura. This is Fitz. I've been trying to contact Julia today, and she has answered none of my calls or text messages. Is everything okay up there? She asked me to come for dinner tonight, something urgent has come up, and I've got to make a quick trip to Texas. She'll understand that it's a business trip. Will you please let her know? I left her a voicemail and a text, but I was afraid she would not get my message. Anyway, I apologize that I can't make dinner tonight. Good-bye."

Straightaway, Roberts sent the recording to the FBI's Department of Forensics, where the message could be examined through the voice activation center. "From there," Roberts explained, "they can determine the caller's location at the time of the call. Measuring his voice's cadence and volume, they can analyze and discover much about the message's sincerity."

He looked over at Laura and said, "This process may take a few moments, but we'll soon have some information about this message."

"Excuse me," Laura asked. "Did you hear something in the voice message that caused alarm? It sounded like a typical message to me. Fitz wanted me to tell Julia that he couldn't make dinner tonight."

He nodded as he read the report from the phone.

"Ma'am. What did you say was the name of the caller, again?"

"His name is Fitz Romano."

"Fitz?" He asked.

"Correct. Fitz is short for Fitzgerald. He was named after President John Fitzgerald Kennedy."

"Where is his family from, ma'am?"

"His mother was born in Colombia. She became involved and married a man from Italy, without her family's blessing. The family ordered a divorce and sent her here for safety reasons. She met someone and had a short fling when she first arrived in the States. She got pregnant, and Fitz is a product of that affair."

Roberts looked a little confused. "So, this Fitz guy, is he Colombian-American or Colombian-Italian? His name is Italian, correct?"

"Yes, his father, although American, was also part Italian. But the Romano name was the name of his mother's husband that her family forced her to divorce when she left Colombia."

He shook his head in confusion, "And, how did you come to know this information about your daughter's boyfriend?"

"Fitz and his mother told me," she explained.

"Thank you, Mrs. Whelchel, for the information," as he sat back down at the conference table.

Andrew said, "Excuse me, Agent Roberts, were there any clues given in the voice message?"

"Yes, sir. But I'm not at liberty to discuss. The Bureau's forensic experts are checking for additional information as we speak."

Chapter Forty-Two

T he truck's speed decreased. There were many stop-and-go movements with sounds that differed from the monotonous humming of vehicles passing on the interstate that lulled them over the past hours. Julia's heart pounded at the thought of being released at the next stop. Although her vision was blurred from dehydration, she could see the time was five o'clock. She was disoriented and didn't know if it was five o'clock in the morning or the afternoon. Julia looked over at her sister and squeezed her hand, and Marsha opened the palm.

Using her index finger, Julia wrote <RELEASE SOON?>

Marsha responded with two nudges from her elbow. Then, she felt her sister's finger on her hand. The next thing she wrote was <FITZ.>

It surprised her when Marsha only nudged one time. As Julia sat in the dark, she wondered what Marsha was thinking. Of course, Fitz would be the one person to contact for help. He was a worldly fellow with friends all over the globe. Surely, he would have a friend in New Orleans for them to stay with until they could find a way back to Georgia.

Remembering that he was due to arrive at the farm for dinner, she wondered if he was already there. Perhaps Fitz and her mother enjoyed a cup of tea while waiting for the girls to return. Fitz would also be a calming influence because she would be livid that they were not home in time to meet with the financial advisor.

Her mother would be even more upset that they hadn't talked throughout the day.

The truck stopped, and then the cab door opened as two of the men walked to the back of the trailer. One of them motioned for the Bottom to unlock the handcuffs, which tied the three of them together.

Julia found the release from her sister's wrist liberating and thought she would send off a text to Fitz as soon as her eyes adjusted to the light. There was water in the bottle sitting between her knees, and she opened the bottle and turned it up and drank it all. She immediately felt better.

There was a discussion between the two men while they looked at their phones and glanced back at the women. They lined up a group of fifteen or twenty girls, and the Bottom led them outside.

In their absence, Julia pulled her phone from her riding boot and typed a quick message to Fitz: <*Sisters and I kidnapped from the barn. In New Orleans. HELP! HELP! Next destination, US Border.*>

The men were only gone for ten minutes when they returned with another group. As the girls were forced into the trailer, they were forced to move back a few feet to allow space for them. The young girls seemed to be around the age of twelve and thirteen, who wore cute clothing and were made up to appear older than their years. They marched single file into the trailer.

Julia reached for Marsha's hand, but Marsha jerked it away when she heard a commotion at the door and watched as the two men entered the back of the trailer. One of them held a large manila envelope that was bulging from the thickness of the contents. The men continued their conversation; they seemed well pleased judging from the animation in their eyes as they walked toward the cab's entrance. The Bottom slammed the door and locked it, and the trailer was dark once again. Julia could feel the air move as the bottom walked past her, and she realized they would not be getting off in New Orleans.

Chapter Forty-Three

A gent Roberts hit the conference table with the side of his fist. "SON OF A BITCH!" he said as he jumped up from the table.

Andrew looked up from his desk and said, "Is there a problem, agent?"

Roberts walked over to the chair he had occupied earlier and told them that the men had missed the deadline. He explained that they were held up in traffic and hadn't made it to the hotel in the French Quarter until half-past five.

"There was a note left inside the room from the captors that explained Houston was their next stop. The note suggested making the exchange in the parking lot across the street from the old Compact Center on the Southwest Freeway. Their ETA is midnight."

Additionally, the note stated that the girls were fine and had experienced no difficulties during the journey. They had also served them meals and offered restroom breaks throughout the trip.

"Thank God!" Laura said. "At least, they are offering them food and a chance to use the restroom. It sounds like they are being treated well."

Roberts whispered to Rhett and Andrew. "I know from experience these people are capable of anything, including selling Mrs.

Whelchel's daughters to a sex trafficking organization, or trading them in a drug deal, if they so desired."

In fact, by now, they could have exchanged the girls several times.

He knew it would be in his best interest not to share this information because Mrs. Whelchel had handled the news from the latest update with such calm.

Roberts sent a text to his office, asking them to speak with the Forensic Department about the voice message from Fitzgerald Romano, recorded on Mrs. Whelchel's cell phone. He insisted that the subject text the results to his phone as opposed to calling.

Turning to Andrew, Roberts said, "I think we should send out for Chinese food. I'm getting hungry, and it looks like we'll be here a while."

Andrew got the order together and asked, "Should I pick up the food, or let the restaurant make the delivery."

"What would you normally do? We don't want to do anything to bring attention to the firm," he replied.

"We would normally have the order delivered to the back door," Andrew said.

"Then, do that. I'll go out back and check out the area." He got up from his chair and looked back at Andrew and said, "Is everyone gone for the day?"

While Andrew read the order to the person on the line, he looked at Roberts and nodded.

Laura closed her eyes as she mumbled.

Andrew hung up the phone and looked hard at Rhett and then cut his eyes to Laura.

"Of course, they're checking every lead. But there's no reason to suspect Fitz." Laura paused as if waiting for an answer. "He would never do that! No, Henry, Fitz loves Julia. He's not involved."

Rhett leaned closer to Laura and said, "Laura, I'll take you home after we eat dinner. Then, I'll return and stay with Andrew and the FBI agent until we get the girls."

"No, Henry. You know I would never leave here until the girls are safe." She reached for Rhett's hand and said, "You understand, don't you, dear?"

Rhett shot a sideways glance to Andrew. Then Andrew quietly got up from behind his desk and walked out the back door.

Roberts looked up when he heard the door close. "What's up?"

"Is it normal for people in these situations to suffer from hallucinations?" Andrew asked. "When you walked out of the room, Laura started talking to her deceased husband, Henry. However, she was looking straight at Rhett as she spoke."

"Yes. We see that kind of behavior a lot. Mrs. Whelchel is trying to control the thoughts going through her mind, which are pretty disturbing, I might add," he paused. "Did she reveal any damaging information while she spoke with her deceased husband?"

Andrew told the agent about the comments about Fitz. He said to him that apparently, Henry's ghost had reservations about the daughter's boyfriend, Fitz Romano.

"When I left the room, I heard her refer to Rhett by name. So, perhaps the conversation with Henry is over for a while. I must admit it was strange."

"Well, we need to keep a watch on her. Make sure she drinks plenty of fluids. This type of mental stress isn't healthy," Roberts said. "Perhaps you should send Rhett a text message, let him know you told me about the conversation. Then ask him to record any further conversations with Henry."

He looked at his phone, "On a separate note, the Bureau has just confirmed they have information linking Fitzgerald Romano to the Suarez Cartel out of Colombia. There's more information, but I'm not at liberty to discuss it with you, Andrew."

"Of course. I wish you hadn't told me about Fitz's involvement with the Cartel. It's bad enough his mom's family owns a company involved in drug activity. But, to think someone like Julia, who I love

214 · RENEE PROPES

like my own daughter, has a boyfriend involved in a drug cartel is hard to fathom."

Roberts lit a cigarette and said, "I can imagine. Given that you're an attorney, I suspect that you've been privy to some rather twisted scenarios during your career. It's unfortunate, but in my line of work, nothing surprises me anymore."

Andrew appreciated the honesty of his cynical remark, "Do you think these incidents are related?"

Still scrolling his phone while puffing a cigarette, Roberts looked up and said, "I'm beginning to think so, yes." He blew smoke up into the air.

"We probably shouldn't mention this piece of news to Laura," Andrew said.

"I agree," Roberts said. "Thank you for keeping this under wraps," he said as he stomped out his cigarette with his shoe. "I'll wait out here for the delivery guy to bring the food."

Chapter Forty-Four

W hen they moved Marsha and her sisters to prepare them for the drop off in Houston, they sat next to the Hispanic girl Marsha had been watching throughout the afternoon. As soon as the door closed, Marsha felt her movement, and she heard, "Perdona." Although Marsha was not fluent in Spanish, she remembered a few words from her college's foreign language class. She recalled "perdona" meant "excuse me."

Marsha smiled, "Do you speak English?"

"Si, senora. Perdona."

"Dear. Are you all right?" Marsha whispered.

"No, senora," she answered.

"My name is Marsha, what's yours?"

"Maria." She whispered.

Marsha reached for her hand and squeezed it as Maria's body shook from the sobs.

When the engine started, and they resumed their journey, the girls' latest addition shifted around on the floor of the trailer as they leaned on each other for comfort. Marsha heard a sweet voice say, "Maria. Is it you?"

Then the young girl shifted closer to them.

"Si. Lucia, I thought it was you."

Marsha repositioned herself and allowed enough room for Lucia to lean on her back. Maria then leaned forward and whispered.

After a few moments, Lucia went off to sleep, and Marsha moved around so the girl's head could rest on Maria's lap.

"Do you know her?" Marsha asked as she pointed to the head of the young girl sleeping on her lap.

"Si, she's my sister."

"How old is Lucia?"

Maria said, "She turned twelve last week. We haven't seen each other in over two years." She cried. "We got separated when she went to a foster home."

"Honey, I'm so sorry. It sounds like you girls have had a tough time."

"Si," Maria said. "You can say that again."

Straining. Julia had heard much of Marsha's and Maria's conversation. She took Marsha's hand and wrote <SISTERS GET OFF AT HOUSTON.>

Marsha wrote back, < GOOD IDEA.>

Maria leaned closer to Marsha and said, "Have you ever been in a place like this?"

"No. The woman in charge told my sisters and me that we would be getting off in Houston. Perhaps we can get you and your little sister off with us," Marsha said.

"That's taking a big chance, isn't it?" asked Maria.

"Yes. We need a diversion to allow you and Lucia to escape when the door opens. We've stopped twice so far, and no one's done a headcount at either stop."

Marsha and Maria whispered back and forth and considered every plausible scenario for their escape. During their discussion, they witnessed a considerable improvement in Maria's English. The younger two girls began to converse in English, too.

Using the light from Julia's watch, they checked Lucia's wrists for signs of branding. There were none, which was very encouraging that she did not belong to a group. In a situation like this, that meant independence, and would make it easier if she chose to run.

When Lucia awakened from her nap, Maria and Marsha told her about their plan to escape. Lucia asked if their cousin, Isabela, could go with them.

"Si," Maria said. "Where is Isabela?"

Lucia pointed to a girl a few feet away.

"I didn't see her with the others," Maria said. "She needs to move closer to us."

Maria looked at Marsha, "Can she come with us? She's our cousin."

Marsha looked at Julia.

"We'd be taking a risk," Julia said.

"I know. But look at them, Julia. They are just children."

Julia nodded in agreement.

Another hour passed before the truck's speed gradually reduced, and then the engine suddenly shut off. Fifteen to twenty minutes passed. When the cab's secret door swung open, two men carrying trash bags entered the trailer and distributed food and water to the girls.

When the men got to the back of the trailer, one of them nodded at Marsha. "You're getting off in Houston. Move your group to the door, now. You'll be the first to exit at the next stop."

Marsha nudged Maria, and then she grabbed Lucia and Isabela's hand and said, "You heard the man, let's go, ladies." Julia and Betsy walked with Maria between them until they reached a small space in front of the door next to Marsha and the two younger girls.

Isabela and Lucia cried because they were afraid one of the other girls would tell the Bottom that they had left their group. Marsha explained that if that happened, and the Bottom asked about it, they should act like they got separated from the others when they climbed into the trailer.

The girls refused to drink their water for fear they would need to use the bathroom.

Julia told them she suspected everyone in the trailer had soiled their clothing and not to worry about the odor. She reminded them that their survival depended upon them staying hydrated, even if that meant drinking the water would cause them to use the bathroom in the trailer.

After another hour listening to the sound of vehicles moving down the freeway, the girls went to sleep. They awoke as the truck slowed for the stop in Houston. Julia's watch showed twelve o'clock.

Chapter Forty-Five

As soon as the truck stopped, the Bottom returned and said to Marsha, "When I unlock the door, you girls should jump out of the trailer as fast as you can. I've got a group of twenty more girls lined up, ready to climb in as soon as the door opens. My orders are to move fast and get them inside the trailer before anyone notices. So, when the door opens, get on out, and you're on your own."

She reached for her key, "Oh, yeah. The boss-man said to tell you that your contact will hold up a yellow sign. Go straight to that sign, and they'll take you to a safe place."

Marsha looked at her group and said, "Okay, girls, get ready to leave. As soon as the door opens, we've got to get the hell out. Do you understand?"

"Si, senora" they said in unison.

Marsha looked at the two younger girls whose lips trembled, and whispered, "Just follow me, and you'll be fine."

When the door opened, they jumped to the ground and rushed away from the trailer. Stopping a hundred feet away, Marsha and the younger girls turned and watched the new group climbing into the back. There was a sudden deafening sound from a helicopter overhead. It appeared to be landing in the vacant parking lot.

Julia walked away from the group to find a signal for her cellphone. She was eager to send off another text to Fitz. Finally, she got a signal. <WE'RE IN HOUSTON. AFTER MIDNIGHT. PLEASE HELP!>

As the chopper set down, a white van rounded the corner, and the brakes screeched as it came to an abrupt stop. The doors opened, and two men jumped out, grabbed the girls, and shoved them into the back. When Julia looked up from her text, she screamed for the van to stop. But the van sped off down a side street and was soon out of sight. As she watched, Julia realized the appearance of the white van had interrupted the exchange.

Julia turned and saw the trailer door shut, and then the tractor-trailer pulled off in the other direction. Suddenly, Julia wanted the truck to stay behind. At least inside the truck, she and her sisters were together. Now they were separated, and she didn't know where they were going.

Realizing something unplanned had just happened, Julia turned toward the chopper, remembering the Bottom's brief instructions before their release. Then, a man descended the steps, holding a yellow sign. He hurried onto the blacktop parking lot while pulling a piece of black luggage. When he reached Julia, she explained what had just happened. She kept pulling at his arm. Julia sobbed as she pointed toward the street and told him they had to go after the van.

The agent rushed Julia into the chopper and they took off in the direction the van was traveling. Using their spotlights, they were able to find the van and follow it to the freeway. Upon leaving the residential areas, they shouted orders from the state-of-the-art loudspeaker system, which could magnify to reach up to a five-mile radius.

The van refused to stop.

The SWAT team pilot noticed another chopper approaching their airspace. When the massive chopper lights came on, it illuminated a far more substantial area, which was helpful. The SWAT team made an immediate circle to the front of the van and made pictures of the men sitting in the front. As instructed earlier, the camera transmitted all images back to the headquarters in Washington.

The forensic lab would search their system to identify the men driving the van. As soon as the picture came up on the screen, the SWAT team radioed Agent Roberts.

"We know that man, sir."

"Forward the pictures to forensic immediately," Roberts said. "It's their responsibility to identify the men. It's our job to stop them."

Chapter Forty-Six

The men pushed and barked orders as the girls crammed into the back of the beat-up van. When they secured the door, the driver jumped in and sped off down a narrow street toward the freeway.

The person in the passenger's seat struggled to close his door as they rounded the curve. Then he turned around, faced the girls, and grew agitated when he saw the younger girls were crying.

"We don't have time to listen to a bunch of crying children," he said as he looked at the older females. "Keep them quiet, or you'll force me to do something unpleasant."

Marsha looked at Betsy, and they each grabbed one of the younger girls and began to rock them back and forth while whispering into their ears. Soon the crying stopped as they continued to cradle them in their arms.

Marsha whispered so both Lucia and Isabela could hear. "Girls, we'll be fine, okay. Just try to quiet your minds for a few more moments."

Lucia looked at her and said, "How do we do that?"

"Think about a special time in your life. Perhaps the day you bought that pretty dress you love or a favorite birthday present you received. Think of a happy memory that brings a smile to your face."

"We don't buy pretty dresses, and we don't get any birthday presents," Lucia said.

Marsha looked at Betsy with surprise.

Chapter Forty-Seven

A gent Roberts received a text and went back to the conference table, punched in an exclusive number, and waited.

There was a sudden beep.

The screen showed an older white van traveling at a high rate of speed down the freeway. The chopper got close enough to read the license plate of the vehicle. He texted the information to his contact in Washington and continued to watch the video.

Then the chopper flew around to the front of the van and took a close-up video of the driver. The camera focused on the inside of the van but could see no one in the back. When the camera shifted to the left, there was a clear picture of the man on the passenger's side.

"THAT TRAITOR!" Roberts yelled as he shook his head in anger.

Laura said, "That man looks familiar. Do you know him, Agent Roberts?"

"Yes, ma'am. Unfortunately, I do."

As the video progressed, a head emerged from the back, and a woman's face appeared on the screen. Laura cried, "Oh, my God! That's our Betsy!"

The video then shifted to the other chopper whose lighting system had allowed the clear pictures of the van and the men.

Roberts got the identification numbers from the side of the van and texted it to forensics. Then he noticed the pilot of the second chopper lifted the position of his aircraft by several thousand feet and circled the airspace as he continued to spotlight the van from the air.

"FBI – SAIC Roberts to SWAT-Air Division. Over," he said.

"Yes, sir, copy," the pilot responded.

"We have identified the other chopper as part of the Suarez Cartel from Colombia. Over."

"10-4 copy. Over."

"The driver of the white van and his associate sitting on the passenger's side are considered armed and dangerous, so be careful. They're considered persons of interest by the Bureau, and you should apprehend immediately."

"Sir, with your permission, since there are five hostages on board, can we shoot the van's tires?"

"Okay. But don't take any unnecessary risks. Your job is to land quickly and grab the two men. We've got another chopper en route now to pick up the ladies," Roberts said.

"I see them on the radar. As soon as the chopper gets closer, I'll let you know."

"Copy that, it's your call, pilot," Roberts said.

"Okay, we're proceeding, sir."

****

"Mrs. Whelchel, we're about to rescue your girls. Julia is in the chopper, and I've just received a confirmation that Marsha is believed to be in the back of the van with Betsy."

"Agent Roberts, can I speak to Julia?" Laura asked. "I just want to hear her voice."

"Maybe soon. Let us focus on getting your other two daughters right now."

Laura walked around Andrew's office and thought about the dangerous situation in which her girls had become involved. It upset her that she didn't prevent the girls from going to the barn. Lord knows, they forewarned her of the potential danger involved.

As she stood at the window, looking up at the stars, she felt the nightmare was about to end, she could feel it in her bones. Hopefully, by morning, her girls would be back at home.

Laura turned and looked over at Rhett, who had not left her side throughout the twelve-hour ordeal. He must have felt her gaze because he got up and walked over to where she was standing.

She placed her hands on his cheeks. "Thank you, Rhett," she said. "You've been a loyal friend throughout all of this. I don't know how I could've gotten through it without you by my side."

"Well, Laura. I have a confession to make."

She tilted her head and said, "What kind of confession, Rhett?"

"The first time I laid eyes on you, I knew that you were someone special. I realize you and Henry were married for a long time, but he's gone now. I'm here, and I'm not going anywhere. When you're ready, I would like to continue this relationship and see what our future together might become."

Without the thought of anyone else being in the room, she leaned over and kissed Rhett on the lips and said, "Well, let's get my girls home first."

Chapter Forty-Eight

T he helicopter pilot for the SWAT team ordered the driver of the van to stop the vehicle. Instead, the driver increased his speed. Finally, the pilot alerted Julia that they planned to open the side door far enough to shoot the van's tires.

"Ma'am, is your seatbelt buckled?" He asked.

"Yes. Of course."

"I'm Agent Johnson, I need you to stay in your seat, and keep the belt engaged until I tell you otherwise."

Then he turned to his partner and said, "We're about to circle out, so the driver will think he lost us, then we'll swoop down, and you shoot the tires. As soon as we see his speed decelerate, we'll land and grab the men first."

"What about the woman in the back here?"

The pilot turned to Julia and said, "Our special trained sniper, who I believe is concerned about your safety, is Agent Tillman. So, let's reassure him, you will stay in your seat with your seatbelt strapped, right?"

Julia rolled her eyes and nodded.

He smiled at the thought of her beautiful eyes.

Johnson returned his focus to the control panel. "Okay, Tillman. Let's do this!"

He lifted the helicopter to the left and swung the aircraft around and flew in the opposite direction.

Agent Tillman was watching the van and said, "Sir, we may have a problem. The van just exited the freeway."

"No worries, man. We'll go out farther. Just monitor the movements of the vehicle."

"There it is," said Tillman. "He's just pulled into the parking lot of that convenience store."

"I'm on it. Get in position."

As the chopper circled around the air space, Johnson saw the lights from another aircraft approaching the target from the opposite direction.

"Who the hell is that?"

"Do you see what's happening?" Tillman yelled. "That chopper's landing at the store." He pulled out his binoculars and recognized the massive Sikorsky S-92 aircraft, which belonged to the drug cartel.

"Oh, crap! Sit tight." Johnson said as he raised the nose of the chopper and made another loop. "Now, we must rethink our approach. Can you determine how many people are in that chopper?"

"Someone just got out of the aircraft and is approaching the side of the vehicle," Tillman said. "There appeared to be only two people in the chopper. The pilot, who just got out, is talking to the guy pumping the gas. The other guy from the van just went into the convenience store."

"How about the second person in the chopper," Johnson asked. "can you see him?"

"No."

It concerned Agent Johnson, that even though it was two o'clock in the morning, a random customer could pull into the parking lot for gas. They spent a few moments discussing their options, but soon realized this would be an excellent time to take them all out and get the girls.

****

"Well, well, well. Look who we have here," Nic Suarez said as he approached the man pumping gas. "If it's not the one and only, Special Agent Bowen, the traitor himself. Wonder what the big boys in Washington will do with you now?"

He looked inside the car window.

"I hear you've got the girls. Where's the suitcase?"

Bowen diverted his gaze back to the gas hose. "What are you doing here, Nic? We told you we could handle this mission."

The guy from the cartel slapped Bowen's head as he grabbed the gas nozzle and returned it to the pump, "Yeah, well, no wonder you never made it to the Washington Bureau. This should have been a straightforward mission, Bowen. All you had to do was pick up a suitcase full of cash in exchange for three females. We've been tracking your movements since you picked up the girls. I hope you realize you left one girl standing in the parking lot across from the old Compaq Center."

"We were getting ready to make the exchange, and you're the one that blew the operation," Bowen said.

"Your timing was off," Nic said. "As usual, you ignored my instructions and were five minutes too late. You should have been waiting in the parking lot when the tractor-trailer got there."

Bowen looked sheepish and dropped his head.

"So, I'll ask you one more time, Bowen. Where is the suitcase?"

"They never gave us the suitcase, Nic. But we got the girls. Look for yourself, they're in the back of the van."

"I don't want the girls, Bowen!" Nic said, "I want the damn money."

Nic pointed to the sound of the chopper in the air. "What is all of this air traffic? Man, are you being followed by your buddies from the FBI?"

Abruptly, he smashed Bowen's head against the van. Although Bowen was almost unconscious, Nic continued to hold him up as a shield.

****

"Men. The Suarez Cartel helicopter is on the scene." Roberts said to the guys in the backup chopper approaching the target. "First and foremost, make sure those girls are safe and then take out the guys sitting up front in the van. You've got pictures for references, in case you're not sure about their identities."

The guys looked at each other, and one man shook his head and said, "Sir, those are two FBI agents. I recognize Agent Bowen, from an earlier assignment and I'm sure Agents Tillman and Johnson have, also,"

Roberts explained that the guys they recognized as FBI agents were now considered persons of interest by the bureau and were suspects in aiding the cartel.

"Gentlemen," Roberts said. "The other guy is Nic Suarez, a high-ranking member in the cartel. Apprehend Mr. Suarez, but don't kill him, unless you can't avoid it. I want him alive. I've just briefed the lead chopper, and he is hovering around the air space, awaiting further instructions. I want you guys to shut off your lights and approach them from behind the store. There's an empty parking lot behind that convenience store where you can land. I have instructed the lead chopper to do the same."

The aircraft lights went off, and they navigated their way to the empty lot behind the convenience store.

As soon as they landed, the two men jumped to the ground carrying MP5 machine guns. They moved toward the van's back door as Robert's voice came through their Bluetooth devices programmed for individual assignments.

"Remember, priority one is to get those girls out safely. And just so you know, besides saving the girls, you're about to bring down one of the world's largest drug operations."

Chapter Forty-Nine

W hen the back doors opened, the large helicopter's lights parked behind the van, blinded the girls' vision. As their eyes adjusted to the bright light, they heard several loud swoosh sounds. Apparently, someone from the massive chopper used a silencer on his firearm and shot the two FBI agents approaching the back of the van.

The first guy landed face-first inside the van.

The girls screamed, and then jumped to avoid the blood that splattered inside. The second guy fell onto the pavement.

Without any understanding from where the shots came, another swoosh sounded, which took out the driver as he walked out of the store with his gun aimed at the van. The next shot hit Bowen in the head, killing him instantly.

Johnson then snuck around behind the cartel's chopper and approached the van just as he saw Nic reach for his boot. He fired a shot, which penetrated his leg. Johnson ran to his side, pushed him onto the ground with the machine gun held to his head as he reached, and grabbed the handgun from his boot.

Tillman then jumped into the passenger's seat of the van.

He turned and addressed the back of the van, "How many of you are back there?"

"There were six of us, but my sister got left at the parking lot in Houston."

"Ma'am, your sister's okay. We picked her up, and she's in our chopper behind the store."

Johnson then spoke to his sniper through his Bluetooth device, "Will your weapon penetrate the windshield of that S-92 aircraft?"

"No, but I've got an explosive device that will do the trick," answered Tillman.

"Do you have it on you?"

"Yep," he answered and then turned to the girls in the back. "Is everyone okay?"

Lucia said, "I'm hungry."

"I know, sweetie," Marsha said. "We'll get some food soon. Let's be quiet."

"Let me out," Lucia cried. "We are all going to get killed."

Marsha grabbed and held her in her lap as she rocked her back and forth like a small child. "It's okay, sweetie. It's okay. The shooting has stopped. They've got the bad guys."

Hearing the child's remark, Tillman looked at Marsha.

"Sir," Marsha said, "these girls probably have eaten very little in days."

"We'll take care of that in a minute. But first, I'm going to climb on top of the convenience store and destroy that chopper behind us. This explosive device is deafening, so cover your ears."

He looked around as he made his way to the back of the store. There was a 10-foot ladder attached to the end of the building that he scaled with rapid speed. Once on top of the building, he looked out across the landscape. Seeing no one within more than a hundred yards of the property and noticing the fuel tanks positioned away from the building, he accessed his weapons.

Although he had anti-personnel grenade shrapnel in his arsenal, he decided that his best course of action was to shoot out the two GE turboshaft engines with incendiary bullets. The high-explosive armor-piercing ammunition created a massive explosion.

Fortunately, the underground fuel tanks were on the other side of the store. And, since it was after two o'clock in the morning, there were no other customers in the parking lot.

After he blew up the engines, he didn't stick around to watch the burning machine. The sniper shimmied back down the ladder and ran to where the pilot held Nic on the ground.

"Slowly, place your hands behind your back and lift to your knees."

Johnson released enough pressure for Nic's arms to move to his back as they secured his hands with zip-ties.

"Okay. Good," Tillman said, "Now slowly stand and walk to the chopper on the other side of the building. We need to get those wounds on your hand and ankle treated."

Tillman stopped and checked the dead guys' pockets, looking for keys to the helicopter, their Bluetooth equipment, or any other items of interest. He grabbed their machine guns and followed Johnson and their captive to the aircraft.

When they got in the chopper, they left Nic's hands behind his back as they wrapped the wound. They wrapped his right ankle and then placed a tracer on his left. Tillman nodded at Johnson as the engine started, confirming that he, too, had received the instructions about their last destination.

"Are you good to go?" Tillman asked.

Johnson nodded, closed the door, and went back to the van to check on the girls.

Chapter Fifty

W hen Agent Johnson returned to the van, he unlocked the vehicle's side door and helped the girls out onto the parking lot.

"We've got a long trip ahead of us, so go into the store and get some snacks to eat on the way back. I'll be in there in a moment to pay the cashier."

He turned and waved to the cashier and pointed to the girls. The cashier nodded in approval.

Then Johnson walked around the burning helicopter and noticed that someone had opened the hatch underneath the aircraft. The glowing metal was too hot to touch. He looked out into the dark night.

I wonder if the force of the explosion caused the trapdoor to open automatically, or if there was someone else in the chopper who used it as an escape exit.

He turned and walked inside the store, and asked the clerk if he had a fire extinguisher. The clerk removed one from the wall and handed it across the counter.

"Have you called the fire department and the police yet?"

"Yes, I called 911, and they are on their way. Also, an ambulance should be here any second, now."

"Okay. Thanks. I'll spray the chopper with this extinguisher."

Johnson looked around at the girls picking out items from the candy aisle. "Are they bothering you?"

"Heck no. The girls are fine. Go, do what you need to do. They can stay in here until you're ready for them to go."

The fire department arrived and finished putting out the rest of the fire. When the local police department finished writing up their report, Agent Johnson went back into the store.

"A tow truck will be by shortly to take that van to the pound. We've arranged for another truck to get the burned chopper, and take it to a military base."

Johnson watched the girls as they clung to their bags of food. Nodding toward them, he asked, "How much damage did they do?"

The cashier smiled, "the total comes to eighty-seven dollars and sixteen cents."

"Thanks, man, sorry we made such a mess out there," Johnson said. "We'll send in a crew to clean up the parking lot immediately."

"Man, I can't believe you blew up that badass machine."

"Yeah, well. That's one perk of being a sniper with a SWAT Team. As a pilot, I seldom get to do the fun stuff. It was a pretty impressive show, wasn't it?"

"Better than fireworks on the Fourth of July," said the cashier.

The pilot laughed.

"Okay, girls. Does everyone have enough goodies to last the trip? If so, let's get into the chopper, and head to Georgia."

As they left the store, Johnson asked, "Did any of you happen to get me a snack?"

Isabela hugged his waist and said. "No. But you can have half of my candy bar because you saved my life."

"Well, thank you, little lady," he chuckled. "That hug made it all worthwhile."

Johnson opened the chopper door and lifted the younger girls inside. He then dropped the ladder and assisted Marsha and Betsy before climbing in himself.

"Okay. We have a few things to discuss before we fly out of here," Johnson said. "First of all, I want you to know that you are now safe."

Isabela's enormous eyes filled with tears, and her bottom lip quivered.

"It'll take us several hours to get home," Johnson said. "So, relax and enjoy your snacks. Take a nap if you like."

There was a look of fear on Isabela's face as she looked outside the aircraft.

"What's your name, sweetie?" Johnson asked.

"Isabela." She said as she wiped her nose with her sleeve.

"Isabela," he repeated. "That sure is a pretty name. Are you going to be okay?"

Shaking her head, vigorously, "just let me out. I've never *volado* before, and I'm scared."

Marsha reached for Isabela and said, "Honey, you'll be fine, flying is fun. You'll get to see the lights from the city as we fly over. Come, sit on my lap, and enjoy your food. When you're done, you can sleep in my lap. Before you know it, we'll be home."

"I don't have a *casa*," she sobbed as tears streamed down her face.

"Yes, you do. You're going home with us."

As Isabela moved closer to Marsha, he knew she would be okay.

Then, Johnson turned to Julia and said, "How did you enjoy the fireworks display we put on this evening, ma'am."

Julia rolled her eyes playfully.

Grinning, he said with a wink, "do that again."

He tossed a bag over to her. "I got you a candy bar and a bottled water. But, you'll have to split that candy bar with me."

He winked at her, then he turned around in his seat and started the engine and yelled, "Three, two, one... lift-off!"

After the younger girls finished their snacks, they snuggled up to Marsha and Betsy and slept.

Julia remained in the same seat and listened to Johnson's conversation with the air traffic control tower. She then leaned forward and watched the instrument panel of the helicopter. "What is that large blue instrument to the left?" she asked.

"Why don't you move up here and be my copilot. You'll be able to watch the panel at a closer range."

"Are you sure it's okay?" Julia asked.

"Of course."

She settled into the seat next to him.

"Hi, my name is Rodney Johnson. My friends call me Rod."

"I'm Julia."

They talked about the instrument panel and the poor connection to the air traffic control tower. Johnson turned to Marsha and Betsy and smiled as he looked at the younger girls sleeping.

When they reached a comfortable altitude, Rod relaxed a bit. But he noticed Julia was on edge. He hated for her to spend several hours in a chopper in a state of anxiety.

"Tell me about your experience today, Julia. I understand they took you in a tractor-trailer from your parents' barn."

Julia started from the beginning and told him about their decision to get up early and go to the barn to determine if their mother had suffered an accident while riding her horse.

Then she told him about the kidnapping at the barn and riding in the trailer with the shrink-wrapped marijuana packages. When she got to the part about being moved to the second trailer, Rod got really interested.

"Wait a minute. The kidnappers moved you and your sisters to another trailer, is that correct?"

"Yes," Julia said.

Then, she told him about the ride with the other females and how they came to know Maria, Lucia, and Isabela. Julia explained how easy it had been to sneak the younger girls out of the trailer, because the men transporting the girls, and the lady who served as the supervisor in the back, were oblivious to them other than to provide food and drink.

"I apologize that we smell so bad," Julia said. "But as you can imagine, our captors didn't allow for bathroom breaks."

"Would you like me to touch down in the next city so you ladies can get some new clothes?"

"No, but thanks. We'll be home soon enough."

"This may seem like a strange question, Julia. You didn't happen to get the tag number of the truck hauling those girls, did you?" Rod asked.

"When I jumped off the back of the trailer," Julia said. "I walked around trying to get a cell signal. As soon as I got one, I took pictures of the trailer's side and back as it pulled out of the parking lot. Interestingly, it looked the same as the first truck that hauled the marijuana."

"How long were you in the second truck?" Rod asked.

"We transferred to the second trailer after a couple of hours, but it was before getting to New Orleans. I'll never forget the stench as we entered the second trailer."

She shook her head in disgust.

"I can imagine."

"We rode in that germ-infested trailer all the way to Houston, Texas," Julia said. "There was hardly enough room to move around in the back because we were packed in there like sardines with perhaps a hundred or more girls. I never knew much about the sex trafficking business, but apparently, it crosses all socio-economic levels. The apparent common denominator to me was age. At each stop, the age of the girls who boarded got younger. The girls lacking in self-confidence seemed to make up the majority."

She explained that Marsha struck up a conversation with Maria.

"Amazingly, at the next stop, Lucia and Isabela got on board then. Maria and Lucia are sisters, and Isabela is their cousin. Marsha and I decided we were going to save that family of girls."

"My God! What a story. So, you and Marsha just decided to sneak the girls off the truck? That was a gutsy move. I'm sure you didn't stop to think how dangerous that was, and how easily you could have been killed."

"Well, we come from a close-knit family, and we just couldn't leave those three behind to become involved in that kind of lifestyle. Our father was a criminal attorney, and we grew up hearing about justice for all people. Honestly, our dad would have expected us to try to save all those girls. Believe me, we would have, if we could've figured out a way to transport them all back to Georgia."

"Send me a copy of the pictures you took," Rod said. "I'll forward them to the office in Washington. Perhaps they'll put a team on their trail."

Rod sent the pictures to SAIC Roberts. Then, he called him on the phone and relayed the story that Julia had told him about the number of girls crammed in the back of the trailer traveling to the US border.

"What's your location now, Johnson?" Agent Roberts asked.

"We're leaving the Nacogdoches air space, sir."

"I'll dispatch a unit immediately. However, head on back to the interstate and see if you can find the truck in question."

"Sir, I have the six females on board we rescued earlier in Houston. Agent Tillman has the guy from the cartel in his chopper."

"Agent, how are the girls?" Roberts asked.

"Their tummies are full of junk food, and they're sleeping right now. You know kids are so resilient. I believe they'll be fine, for now. But when this is over, they'll need counseling."

Roberts insisted he turn and head back toward the interstate until he could get another SWAT team dispatched from the Houston area.

Rod hated to add flight time to the trip because he knew the girls were eager to return home and get cleaned up.

However, like Roberts, he couldn't allow over one hundred girls to arrive at the border and be sold into trafficking, either. At least, the girls couldn't be harmed while locked in the chopper.

Rod turned to Julia and told her about the change in plans. "I know you ladies want to go home, but we seldom get lucky enough to stop a trailer full of young girls before they reach the border."

Julia reached over and patted his bicep and smiled.

"Thank you! It's been bothering me that we escaped, and the other girls' lives were about to be ruined. Rod, you wouldn't believe, but most of those kids got on the trailer drugged so badly, they hardly knew to put one foot in front of the other. Some of them evidently hadn't bathed in weeks, and although they offered them food and drink, they weren't aware enough to care."

Rod explained that he would increase the speed a bit to gain time. As soon as he reached the freeway near Houston, he turned on the spotlight to search for trucks with signage like the picture Julia had provided.

"What compelled you to take that picture, Julia?"

"I don't really know, Rod. When the van pulled off, I was so upset and didn't know what to do. There was this one moment when I finished texting, as I was trying to process what was happening, that I thought I should get a picture of the tractor-trailer just in case."

"Without the picture," he said, "it would be like looking for a needle in a haystack."

"Well, I just hope we can find the one truck with a star on the trailer's back doors," Julia said.

"I know," Rod said. "The star serves as a signal to other traffickers that they are headed to the US Border. It took a while for our intelligence to determine the significance of that solid blue star."

The radio beeped, and Rod said, "Hold on, copilot. Let's get our next set of instructions."

"Johnson are you there?" Roberts asked.

"Yes, sir. Copy that."

"The SWAT Team is in the air. When they reach your airspace, they will ride alongside you for a few miles. Then we'll release you to continue your flight to Georgia. Stay on course until you hear otherwise."

"Copy that."

Julia looked at Rod and noticed the firm outline of his face. He had dark blonde hair and medium complexion, and like her father's eyes, his were dark brown and spoke to her. She smiled and remembered a conversation with her mother about girls' attraction to men like their fathers. First, Fitz, and now, here sits Rod, with the same height, build and eye color as her dad.

"What are you smiling about?" Rod asked.

Julia shrugged and looked out the window so he couldn't see her face. As she watched the aircraft's twinkling lights, she became relaxed enough to enter a dreamlike state as her thoughts returned to her relationship with Fitz.

We were not a good fit.

There was the money she had found in the suitcase, and the package of cocaine he had sent to her mom's house.

He had carelessly placed her in a dangerous situation which could have caused a felony charge. A possible arrest which would have resulted in her losing her job and spending time in prison.

Furthermore, there was the remark his mother made at the hospital, about them not being evenly yoked. Julia wasn't sure why his mother felt compelled to make that comment. As she thought about his mom's remark, she felt a shiver discharge through her body.

The sound of the radio jarred her thoughts. Then Julia remembered when she was in the chopper waiting for Rod and Agent Tillman to apprehend the drivers of the van. And she thought she recognized Fitz in the back of the cartel chopper. She panicked when she believed the helicopter explosion captured Fitz inside the aircraft.

But a few moments after the burst, she saw Fitz walking to the side of the convenience store towards the wooded area in the back. He could have been just an ordinary guy wearing a black baseball cap and a black jacket, but his gait drew her attention.

As she thought about the moment, she knew it was Fitz. At that moment, he was so close to the helicopter she could have reached out and touched him. Had he just lifted his head up toward the window as he passed, he would have seen her watching from inside the chopper. However, Fitz had not looked up at the helicopter, but had kept a low profile while looking at the ground.

She remembered watching him disappear behind the store, knowing that it was because of their relationship that someone had kidnapped her and her sisters.

Julia wiped her eyes when she heard Rod speaking into the radio to Carl Dawkins, the SWAT team pilot from the helicopter flying near them.

Agent Dawkins said, "I hear you've got three women onboard your aircraft."

Rod laughed and said, "Well, I hesitate to tell you, there are three women and three young girls flying with me tonight."

"You always were one lucky bastard."

"Yeah, it's true. I can't deny that fact."

"Don't go falling in love, we got a job to do," Dawkins said.

"Too late," Rod said as he winked at Julia. "I've already moved one up to the copilot seat to help me navigate the airspace."

"Excuse me. Do you see that line of trucks ahead of us?" Dawkins asked.

"Copy that. We should separate now and fly to the side of the freeway. We're looking for a blue star in the middle of the back door," Rod said.

"Copy, over." Agent Dawkins ventured off to the right and adjusted his light for better vision.

Rod stayed on course and reduced his altitude. "Julia, how well can you see the rear end of those rigs on the freeway?" Rod asked. "There's a pair of night-vision glasses in that side pocket if you need them."

"I have a clear view," she said. "The D.O.T. numbers are visible from here."

"Tell me when you spot a blue star, please."

"Will do." Julia turned and concentrated on each rig as they flew over them.

Rod explained that when they spotted the truck, one helicopter would hover above the vehicle, and another would fly close enough for the driver to see him. They would use the speakers to instruct the driver to pull over. Julia and Rod decided the nearest US border port would be Progresso, Texas, about a four-hour trip from their current location.

Julia had never seen so many tractors on an interstate. They lined as far as the eye could see, and many of the rigs were white, with very few markings on the trailer's exteriors.

They talked about the documentary Julia, and her sisters had watched after her father died. When she finished relaying the information she'd learned from the television program, she said, "You know, it's like God was preparing us for this situation. Had we not watched that documentary, we would've had a clue about what was happening. Of course, we would have figured it out eventually, but as soon as they moved us into the second trailer, and we saw the brokenness of those girls, we knew our destination point."

"Did your captors try to drug you ladies?" Rod asked.

"No. The only drugs they exposed us to were marijuana blocks covered in brown paper and shrink-wrapped in the first trailer. There must be a machine somewhere that presses the marijuana into uniform blocks for transporting."

"How much marijuana would you estimate you saw?"

"Goodness, the trailer was full. There were perhaps ninety to a hundred pallets in that trailer."

Julia sat up in her seat and watched the row of white rigs traveling under the chopper. She thought that her eyes were playing tricks on her when she counted three trailers with the blue star on the back doors. She looked over at Rod, "Do you see that? Three rigs are fitting the description in the picture, one of which is our guy."

"How can you tell?" asked Rod.

"The D.O.T. number matches."

"We just spotted our rig," Rod said. "Three white tractor-trailers are traveling in a row, all of which have the same marking on the back."

"Okay. I see the trucks. How should we proceed?" Dawkins asked.

"Why don't you take the lead on this one? You go out in front. The girls and I will hover over the rig and create a little noise, which should create some anxiety for the driver."

Chapter Fifty-One

A gent Tillman flew into the Andrews Air Force Base near Washington, D.C. and waited for FBI officials to arrive.

Tillman grabbed his phone and texted his contact, careful not to disturb the sleep of his prisoner.

His phone beeped.

The text instructed him to taxi into a hanger close by.

Nic Suarez had fallen asleep during the trip to Atlanta. When the helicopter taxied into the hanger, and the engine cut off, Tillman could hear the steady rhythm of his breathing from the back where he slept.

Knowing the potential consequences of transporting a dangerous drug cartel member, like the Suarez operation, he released a deep breath as the hanger's door closed. Tillman exited the aircraft and locked the chopper. He then lit a cigarette as he walked out the side door to get some air.

Across the landing strip, he noticed a helicopter, identical to the one he'd blown up at the convenience store.

Did the cartel follow my trail?

252 · RENEE PROPES

He inhaled the smoke from the cigarette as he tilted his head and exhaled circles of smoke into the night air.

Agent Tillman looked at his phone and read the message from Agent Roberts, <The Department of Homeland Security will approach the hangar momentarily. Release the prisoner into their custody.>

I better let Roberts know about this helicopter. It might not belong to the cartel, but I can't be too careful.

He dialed Robert's cell number. "Sir, the prisoner was sound asleep when I locked him in the chopper."

"When Homeland gets there, go into the chopper and wake him up. Assist them in removing him from the hanger," Roberts explained. "Be prepared for some resistance."

"Copy that," replied Tillman. "A chopper identical to the one used by the cartel was behind me in the taxiway and is parked on the apron. I've got the aircraft's tail code and modex, if you need to check out the database for identification."

"Yeah, give me the numbers, Tillman," Roberts said. "Until we know for sure about the identification of that chopper, perhaps you should lock the door when you go back into the hangar. Once you wake the prisoner, take him through another area and exit through the back. We should exercise extreme caution until Homeland has him secured inside their vehicle."

"Copy that, sir."

"Those are the most sophisticated and costly helicopters on record. I'm always suspicious when I spot one. We cannot discount the idea that another cartel member stepped up to follow you."

"Sir, is there any word from my pilot?"

"We are in constant contact with Agent Johnson. He's got the girls, and now he's monitoring the freeway for the tractor-trailer involved in the sex-trafficking operation."

"Is he handling the operation solo, sir?" Tillman asked.

"Negative. Shortly after you departed Houston, we dispatched another SWAT team to assist."

Tillman pondered how to express his concern.

"Sir, with all due respect, Johnson is a trained SWAT pilot."

As Agent Roberts checked the database about the identification of the chopper, he sensed Tillman's hesitancy.

"Listen to me, Tillman. Don't worry about it, the guy graduated at the top of his class at West Point, he did two tours in Afghanistan, and two at Quantico. He can handle the job."

Chapter Fifty-Two

A s they listened for updates from the girls, Laura walked around Andrew's office and read the diplomas on the walls. When she came to the bookcase, she recognized the names of a few books on the middle shelf.

Rhett walked over to her and said, "Are you ready to go home?"

"No. I'm going to wait until their helicopter lands, and I know they're back on Georgia soil."

Roberts answered his phone and said to the caller, "Sure, I can go outside." He walked around the parking lot for close to ten minutes.

Laura looked out the window, and she saw Roberts walking around with the cell phone held to his ear. Suddenly, he stopped walking and moved his phone from his right hand to his left, and then he rubbed his eyes. She couldn't hear the conversation, but she thought he looked frustrated.

Laura turned to Rhett and said, "Do you think there's been a new development? Agent Roberts appears disturbed by the phone call he took outside."

Rhett walked to the window, watched the agent for a few minutes, and told her to not get too worked up about it. He explained that he could have been taking a personal call from a family member or perhaps, receiving an update from headquarters about another case.

He placed his arm around her shoulder and said, "Let's go sit on the sofa for a few minutes and try to relax. You can put your head on one end of the sofa, and if you turn sideways, there should be enough room for me on the other end."

Laura lay down on the sofa, as Rhett had suggested. Both were asleep when Agent Roberts came back into the room.

****

Roberts motioned for Andrew to step into the reception area. Then he explained the recent development involving the search for the tractor-trailer that had transported Laura's girls to Houston.

"Andrew," he said. "Perhaps it's best to not mention this latest development to Laura just yet. I don't think we should withhold information if she asks us, but to tell her they were transported in a sex trafficking trailer is a bit much for her tonight, don't you think?"

"But the girls are safe, and traveling in our SWAT chopper, right?" Andrew asked.

"That is correct; however, the pilot was redirected," Roberts said. "The SWAT chopper is now involved in monitoring the traffic on the interstate. They are looking for the truck that's traveling to the US Border to sell the hundred or so young girls to sex trafficking."

"How would they know which truck to search for?" Andrew asked.

"Those girls are clever. Apparently, one of them got a picture of the trailer showing the number registered with the Department of Transportation and a sign on the backdoor that identifies them as a rig used for sex trafficking purposes."

"Dammit," Andrew said. "This plot just gets more complicated as the night progresses."

"True, but if they can stop that truck," Roberts said, "we will save a hundred or so young girls from a lifestyle from which they would never recover. Can you imagine what that will mean for those young girls?" He motioned to the back door, and they walked outside. Agent Roberts looked up into the sky and lit a cigarette.

"I can't even imagine the risk those SWAT team members take each day," Andrew said.

"Well, think about tonight. The SWAT team has saved six females from being sold at the border. They blew up a multi-million-dollar aircraft that is used by a drug cartel, and they captured the leader of the cartel. I don't know if I ever told you, but the million-dollar ransom was never exchanged. It remains in the helicopter with the pilot."

"Let me ask you something. Where did you get the money for the ransom?" Andrew asked.

Roberts placed his hand on Andrew's shoulder and said. "Now friend, I can't be revealing all of my tricks. Let's just say, the Bureau is part of the federal government, and they can print money that looks real but is not legal tender. Does that make sense?"

"Good God! Please, don't tell me anymore. I'll never look at a US Dollar the same," Andrew laughed as he turned and went back inside.

Rhett opened his eyes when he heard Andrew come back into his office.

"Are there any recent developments?" Rhett asked.

Andrew nodded and said, "Try to get some rest. Everything will get hectic once the sun comes up."

Rhett nodded and then looked over at Laura, who was snoring quietly and sound asleep.

Chapter Fifty-Three

Rod and Julia watched as the other SWAT chopper moved ahead and circled in front of the other tractor-trailers. As he circled the airspace, he swept down far enough to get a good visual of the first truck driver, which was the same one that had transported Julia and her sisters.

Static from the radio indicated that Agent Dawkins was about to speak, "Johnson, should I take a few pictures before we stop them?"

Rod looked at Julia and said, "What do you think copilot? Would you like a picture?"

Julia smiled and said, "I would think that taking a picture would be the prudent thing to do before ordering the truck to stop."

"Yes, Dawkins. Let's get a few pictures. Send me a copy when you get a second."

"Copy that. I'm going to mess with the driver's mind a little bit, so be patient."

Dawkins increased his altitude as the truck driver strained his neck to watch his chopper move out of sight. Dawkins flew out in front and approached from another direction and swept down so the driver could get a good look at the helicopter.

The driver wore a baseball cap and had a scruffy beard. His fidgeting made it clear to Dawkins that they'd touched a nerve because he would lift the baseball cap from his head and lower it to cover his bald head. It was a subconscious act, but every time the chopper flew into view, the driver repeated the action.

Rod continued to fly around the truck, and while hovering overhead, he dropped the aircraft within feet of the trailer so the sound from the chopper would deafen the driver. He lowered the aircraft several times, and when the helicopter circled back around in front of the truck, Rod laughed when the driver lifted his finger to Dawkins.

"Rod, we just got the finger from the driver. Perhaps you should back off a little. We don't yet know what kind of dude we're dealing with."

"Copy. Have you heard from your backup unit yet?" Rod asked.

"No. But, I'm going to need a backup, when I order the driver to stop."

"Copy. Let me know when you decide. We'll continue to monitor the other two trucks behind the target. Unless, of course, they stop at the same time, in which case, I'll put it down and lock the girls inside my chopper."

"Copy that. Thanks, man. That's a good plan."

They continued to hover over their target for another hour, and Rod noticed a considerable drop in the fuel gauge since leaving Houston.

Julia must have been paying attention to the fuel instrument and said, "Rod, how do you suppose we're going to get a refill on fuel?"

Nonchalantly, Rod said, "There is a military airport close by, and we'll swing by there and get refueled. I've been waiting for the backup to arrive before I let down. They train us to stay with our assignments until we're replaced by another unit."

"When we stop, I'll need to use the ladies' room," Julia said.

"No problem. There is a restroom in the back. Have you ever been on a houseboat?" He asked.

"Yes, of course," she said.

"Well, the bathroom onboard this thing is like the one you would find on a houseboat. So, you can decide if you want to use it or not." Rod said.

"Thanks. I'll be back in a few."

As Julia returned from the bathroom, she found each of the girls in the back sound asleep.

"I'd really like to talk with Marsha for a minute," Julia said. "But I don't want to wake her."

She sat down in the co-pilot's seat and buckled her seatbelt. "I see we're still in aggravation mode here."

"Yeah. They dispatched a backup from the Houston office, and he should've already been here. I sure hope he shows up before we reach the border," Rod said.

Julia looked at the chopper circling ahead of them, and she panicked when she thought about what would happen if they made it to the border. She closed her eyes and envisioned long lines of vehicles waiting to show papers to the authorities.

"Tell me, Rod," Julia said. "Does every vehicle get searched at the border, or is it a random search?"

"That's a good question, Julia. I'm not one hundred percent sure I know the answer. Although, I've heard reports that the US Customs and Border Protection Agency works tirelessly to guarantee any vehicle is searched that appears to raise suspicions. Of course, they should not allow some vehicles through customs. However, once you visit the operation, you'll have a better appreciation for the agency that handles the border patrol."

Julia looked over at Rod with a look of fear on her face. "Rod, I hope we don't make it to the border. It's almost four o'clock. How much further is it?"

He looked at his instruments, "A little more than an hour," he said.

"Okay," Julia said. "I'm going to rest my eyes for a few minutes. Nudge me if you need my help."

Within moments, Julia had fallen into a deep sleep, and Rod watched the soft rhythm of her breathing. He looked at her beautiful face, and wondered if she had a current love interest.

Rod mused, *A woman like Julia would have a man in her life, or at least she should.*

As he looked around at the back of his chopper, he watched as the others slept. Betsy and Marsha were pretty, too. But there was something special about Julia. Perhaps, it was her demeanor that attracted him to her. She wasn't a silly nervous type that giggled and talked in a high pitch voice. When she spoke, there was a measure of intelligence in her voice that commanded attention. And those beautiful eyes could almost reach out and touch you.

The static from the radio sounded, "Johnson, I just heard from the backup unit. They should reach us within the hour, perhaps just in time for the targeted trucks to get in the long line at the border. I'm going to radio ahead and find out what the traffic is like in that area. I'll get back with you in a few minutes. Over."

"Copy, my girls are sleeping. We're hoping they will remain so as we approach. I'm afraid a trip to the border might spook these girls," Rod said.

"Hopefully, the backup will get here before we arrive. Over."

Rod and Julia spent the next forty-five minutes of the journey in silence. While Julia rested her eyes, Rod tried to develop a plan if the backup didn't make it in time. He made a call to the SAIC, Roberts would call the Pentagon and asked for military assistance.

He suggested bringing in the National Guard to redirect traffic at the border. All eighteen-wheelers will be directed to one lane, and from there, they could isolate the trucks transporting the girls. In the back of the chopper, there was only silence, and the only movement was when one of the girls went to the bathroom.

As they approached the border, the static from the radio started, Agent Dawkins said, "Johnson, my backup is about 30 minutes out. We should perhaps decide how we are going to handle this situation at the border."

"Copy," Rod said. "Perhaps we should notify SAIC Roberts. He should contact the US Customs and Border Protection Agency and ask how they want to handle it. They'll be able to direct the flow of traffic and pull the three tractors aside."

"Do you have a contact to call at the border?"

"Yes," Rod said. "I do. But SAIC Roberts will have his own contact. I'll take care of it and let you know."

Rod searched his phone for the number provided by the Pentagon and radioed ahead. He was told to text him as soon as he was in the airspace above the border, and he would need to fly above the tractor-trailers to target them for inspection.

When the SWAT team was in the area, they would often ask them to fly over the lines and look for suspicious activity. Once the team noticed something out of the ordinary, they would hover over the truck's hood until the agency marked it for inspection.

Dawkins listened to Rod's explanation about what he discussed with his contact at the agency. "The agency uses a device like a paint gun that marks the trucks front window targeted for inspection. Then those trucks get directed to a separate lane. Of course, we need to remember that when the girls exit the truck, they will go into a holding bay at the border until they can get processed through the system. They must get proper medical treatment and go through a detox program, without which the girls can never blend into society."

They had not involved Agent Dawkins in an assignment such as this in the past. He said, "So, although this effort will prevent the girls from being sold into sex slavery, the group will move from the cramped trailer to a holding bay. Is that correct?"

"That's correct," Johnson said. "The potential for getting into a program for re-entry is very promising. Unfortunately, my contact said that most of these girls come from a foster family environment, and may return to the same lifestyle when they get through the detox program. You know, man, we've just got to do a better job instilling confidence in these children. Most of these girls have been on drugs, abused by a family member, or have grown-up in a homeless shelter. And, as a result, their self-esteem is at rock bottom."

"I'm assuming," Dawkins said, "the taxpayers of this country shoulder the burden of the cost for these detox programs, right?"

"That's right," Johnson said. "From the sound of things, the border control is short-staffed. They inspect fewer than ten percent of the trucks that pass through the border. Of course, these truck drivers know this, and they are not as concerned with getting caught as they may have been a few years back. Providing they do nothing stupid; they'll get through the border without notice."

When they were a few miles out, Rod texted his friend at the agency and made their presence known. The National Guard was already on site, halting traffic and directing the eighteen-wheeler trucks into one lane. Using a thin ray of light, they hovered over the three trailers. The agency patrol rode by and marked an area of the window on the passenger side of the truck. Usually, the driver never knew they were being targeted for inspection.

The SWAT Team stayed in the airspace over the border until they pulled over the three trucks for inspection. The agency made an initial assessment and determined they needed the SWAT Team's support in maintaining order, besides the National Guard.

"Listen, man, the agency has asked that we land our choppers on the strip to the right of the holding bay. This is a busy time down here, and they've asked that we lend a hand."

****

Earlier, the sound of the chopper lured Julia to sleep.

One afternoon, Julia drove home following her shift at the hospital to tell her parents about her separation from her husband. They were sitting in the dining room at her parent's house, enjoying dinner. She was a mess as she explained that she'd just made a wrong decision. Although her husband looked like and often acted as her father, he'd proven to be a different person after the wedding, and wasn't reliable.

As her father finished his coffee, he removed his napkin from his lap and laid it to the left of his plate. "Well, sweetheart, I don't consider myself an expert on marriage. But I can tell you this with absolute certainty. Marriage is a crapshoot. There's a fifty-fifty chance, the marriage will work, and you just landed on the wrong side of the playing field."

Her father continued to encourage Julia by explaining her more exceptional attributes. Then he suggested that she ask her husband to leave. He told her she should be the one to stay in the apartment. Most of the wedding gifts and furniture were gifted from their family and friends or purchased by him and Laura.

"If he gives you any flack about that, you let me know."

Julia sobbed as she thought of her imploding marriage. As her mom cleared the dishes from the table, her dad got up from the dinner table, walked into his study, and returned with a decanter of bourbon and two crystal glasses. He poured each of them a drink.

"Now listen to me, young lady. Julia, you are a smart, beautiful, and accomplished woman. Any sane guy would be honored to marry you. One of these days, when you least expect it, the man of your dreams will show up. You may not recognize him at first, because the feeling will be so natural, so familiar. But there he'll be, just waiting to capture your heart. You mark my word, Julia. A charming prince is out there waiting to find you."

265

He pointed his finger at her, "Don't you dare settle for second best again!"

Julie knew her father was paying close attention as she relayed the story of their short two-year marriage. And she also knew that her parents were wondering if their son-in-law had ever struck her. Julia overheard her parents talking after dinner when they thought she was out of earshot.

Her father said, "Laura, I could tell by watching her body movements he'd never hit her. Of all our girls, Julia is the most trusting of the three. But, after listening to her for over an hour, I detected no signs of domestic violence in their marriage."

****

When Julia awoke, she'd listened to the exchange over the radio for a few moments. "Rod, are you going to leave us in the chopper while you go work the detail?"

"Yes. But, trust me, Julia," he said, "I'll lock the chopper and take the keys with me because I don't want you to get away."

He smiled and winked at her.

"Well, don't you think we should tell the others what you're about to do?" Julia asked.

"Sure." Rod said. "Let's wake the girls up and tell them we're about to be in a perilous situation, and they should sit here and watch."

"Laugh, if you want. I'm waking my sisters right now."

Julia removed her seat belt and slid back to the back of the chopper.

Rod could hear them whispering in the back. Still, the radio static and the noise from the trucks inline below the chopper prevented him from hearing what they were discussing.

Until, of course, he heard Betsy scream. She'd been asleep for the entire trip and wasn't aware that they'd redirected their route from Atlanta to the border.

Julia came back to her seat in the cockpit, and Rod glanced over at her.

He waited for a moment.

"Well, how did that work out for you?"

Julia stuck out her tongue and said, "It would've been irresponsible to not tell my sisters about the danger we are about to face, Rod."

"Okay. Well, now they know. But, when I get out of the chopper, you must promise me you will keep the doors locked," he said. "Look around, Julia, there are thousands upon thousands of people in this concentrated area, and if one of those girls gets out of this chopper, we may never find them. My charge is to return you and the others back to your home near Atlanta, and I intend to do just that."

He lifted a strand of her hair and moved it behind her ear. "I've gotten rather attached to you during this mission, and I don't want to lose you."

She stopped her sass.

They landed the choppers, and the other pilot, Dawkins, and Rod got out and locked up their aircraft. With their machine guns in hand, they stood guard while each trailer emptied, and the girls walked single file over to the holding bay.

The drivers of the three tractor-trailers were handcuffed and taken to a holding cell for interrogation.

Rod overheard one official at the border say that those six guys would never again enjoy the light of day.

When the girls filed out, and the trailers completely emptied, 325 young girls were saved from a life-altering experience.

Chapter Fifty-Four

Rod locked the chopper and assumed a position behind the truck, Marsha and Betsy moved to the front of the helicopter to watch as the young girls crawled from the trailers. Their physical appearance and the visibly broken spirit of each girl was appalling.

Betsy became enraged by what she saw, and she was livid that they were moving the girls from one cramped trailer to another crowded holding area. On impulse, she got up from her seat and said, "I can't sit by and let this happen. There must be something we can do to help the process along."

She reached for the door and jumped out before Julia or Marsha realized what she was doing.

Julia jumped up and went back to the door, "Betsy, get back in here! You're going to get killed."

But Betsy kept running toward the holding area as Julia and Marsha sat in the chopper, screaming about their little sister's reckless behavior.

"Rod made me promise that I would keep that door locked once he got out." Julia said. "Of course, Betsy would be the one to do something stupid."

Betsy arrived at the fenced gate where the girls filed into the bays, they watched in horror as a member of the border authority approached their sister. They exchanged a few words, and then Betsy reached for her boot and removed a small handgun.

Julia screamed from the aircraft's cockpit, "Betsy, what in the hell are you doing?"

She turned to Marsha and said, "That impulsive nature of hers will get her in deep trouble one of these days!"

"Daddy always said her impulsive nature would likely be the death of her," Marsha said. "I'm sure he didn't mean it in the genuine sense of the word. However, he said it often enough to make one believe her irresponsible behavior was concerning."

"Where did she get that gun?" Julia asked.

"Well, it looked like she had it in her boot."

The younger girls whispered about the numbers of people being crammed into the holding bays. They were oblivious to the dangerous situation Betsy had gotten into.

Marsha said, "I now remember when Hal bought her that handgun. I forgot all about it."

"I wonder if she even has a permit to carry a firearm?" Julia asked. "I'm not sure she's trained enough to carry a handgun. Oh, crap! It looks like he just grabbed her hands, put them behind her back, and took the gun... Where is he taking her? Oh, my God, he just shoved her into the cage with the others!"

They strained as they watched their sister until she'd ventured deep into the sea of people already in the cage.

Julia turned on the cellphone and saw there was cell service in the area. There was a text from Fitz, where he had responded to her last plea for help. The text message explained that he would make some calls, get them released, and for her to trust him.

She cut off her phone, and then turned her head to the window.

We're done, Fitz, she thought. *I'll never trust you again.*

Julia noticed Marsha was growing more anxious now that Betsy had disappeared into the cage with the other girls. *Poor Marsha, as the oldest child she feels responsible for Betsy's actions.*

Then Marsha mentioned leaving the younger girls in the chopper and going to find Betsy.

"Marsha, what are you thinking? You can't get her out of the cage. We'll have to wait for Rod, and let him use the contacts he's made down there to get her out," Julia said.

"Call me crazy, but I can't stand by and watch my sister locked up in a cage with a bunch of drugged girls on their way to detox. She'll just become another number, Julia!" Marsha exclaimed. "If we don't act now, we may never see her again!"

"Okay. We'll go together. But promise me we won't separate," Julia said.

Marsha told Maria that she was to lock the door to the chopper when they got out and not open the door for anyone except Rod. They also told them to lie down on the floor so that no one could get them. The younger girls started crying, as they wanted to go, too. Their plan especially upset Isabela, but Marsha kept assuring her they would be back as soon as they found Betsy.

Maria took charge of her sister and cousin, "We'll be okay here. But please be careful. What will happen if you don't come back? Where will we go?"

Marsha touched Maria's cheeks, and looked her straight in the eye, "We will return in just a few minutes. Just do as we say, and you will be fine. Please understand, we can't leave our sister out there alone. We have to bring her back to safety."

Julia and Marsha hugged the girls and then stepped out of the chopper and headed toward the cage.

Chapter Fifty-Five

Frustrated and anxious, Marsha and Julia waded through the mass of people until they reached the bay area.

As they approached, Marsha whispered, "Julia, let me handle this, okay?"

"Sure."

A member of the National Guard, who was posted near the fence to prevent unauthorized individuals' access to the site, stopped them.

"Sir," Marsha said, "our sister came into this cage about ten minutes ago, and we need to go in and find her. Will you allow us to enter with the understanding that we will return to you in a few moments?"

"What does your sister look like?" he asked.

"She has blonde hair and brown eyes, and she's about this tall."

The soldier smiled and said, "Ma'am, do you know how many girls fitting that exact description have passed through this gate since I've been on duty?"

Marsha realized the logic in what he said, "But it would be obvious that our sister isn't a girl picked up on the streets."

"With all due respect, ma'am, why would I think she wasn't one of the hundred other girls who have passed through the gate already today?"

"Well, for one thing, she's dressed well." Then Marsha looked down at her own outfit and smiled at the absurdity of her remark. "Of course, we don't look any better, and I'm sure we smell as bad as anyone here, right?"

The soldier asked Marsha and Julia to step over to the side, and he waved for someone to relieve him of his duties. When the replacement arrived, he directed Marsha and Julia away from the cage.

They told him about the ordeal they had been through over the past twenty-four-hour period. The story intrigued the soldier, and he agreed to let one of them go into each cage to look for Betsy.

"Sir, we'd prefer to go in together."

"Suit yourself," he said. "But you'll cover more ground if you separate."

Marsha went into the first bay while Julia took the second. They agreed to meet back outside at the end of thirty minutes to update each other of their progress.

When Marsha entered the bay, she realized there were more people there than they saw from the chopper. There were girls of all ages, including girls much younger than the teenagers they had seen in the back of the trailer in which they had traveled.

As Marsha made her way through the holding cell, she noted many young mothers were holding infants in their arms while their young children clung to each leg.

Some girls were sitting on the concrete pad, while others sat against the chain link fencing. Still others were walking around, talking to anyone who would listen to their story.

The border control employees were all dressed in uniform and carried a backpack. The staff members regularly stopped to reprieve a pouch or pamphlet or bottle of water from the bag. They were generous with the supplies they carried, often giving children individual packs of crackers and candy.

Marsha recognized one of the staff who Betsy had pulled the gun on, and she stopped and asked him about the situation. He shrugged his shoulders and pretended that he didn't know what she was talking about.

She continued to wade through the army of people until she noticed someone sitting in the corner of a section surrounded by little children. She knew it was Betsy because she recognized the riding pants and boots. Betsy sat on her folded legs, and she covered her ears with her hands.

Marsha opened the door, which had been left unlocked. When she looked around at the little children on the floor, her heart broke. Although they were in a safe section of the bay, their faces were filled with fear. It was apparent the separation from their parents marked their long-awaited arrival at the border. The chances of them being reunited with their families would take some time.

As she looked at their beautiful faces, she thought: *Oh, how I would love to take these kids back to Georgia. I would adopt a few of them and foster the others to my friends who could raise another child.*

Gradually, she made her way to the corner of the section and knelt next to Betsy. As soon as she looked at her, she knew that Betsy was sedated, because of her previous outburst. Marsha reassured Betsy in a low voice, but it created no response. Betsy simply turned her head away from Marsha and placed her head against the chain-linked fence.

Marsha tried to lift Betsy from the ground, as she explained that she needed to stand up and return to the chopper. She pulled her sister to her feet and turned toward the entrance of the cage, but Betsy's legs would not support her weight, and she fell back down to the ground.

Marsha looked around in search of someone to help her. She wondered what Julia was doing roaming around the next cell and thought it would be nice to get a message to her sister, although she had no way to do so other than by foot.

She sat down next to Betsy and put her arm around her and spoke in a slow but soft voice. All the while, Betsy shook uncontrollably, and Marsha knew she needed to get word to Julia. She told Betsy that

276 · RENEE PROPES

she was going over to the other cage to get their sister and would return to get her. Marsha continued to hold Betsy until she fell into a deep sleep.

****

Betsy was in the labor and delivery area, waiting to give birth to her first child. The contractions, although five minutes apart, caused unbearable piercing pain. She screamed and shook and begged Hal for meds.

"Please, Hal! Get them to give me something for this pain!"

Several hours passed, and Betsy was almost in a state of hysterics.

"Listen, Betsy," Hal said. "I'm going out to the waiting room to talk to our parents. They need to know that we are getting close to the time of delivery."

As he turned to leave, Betsy grabbed his arm.

"Get my mom in here. I want my mama now! She'll know what to do."

Within minutes, the door to Betsy's room opened, and Laura and Henry walked in behind Hal. As soon as Betsy saw them, her tantrum increased to a level none had ever witnessed.

Henry went around to the other side of the bed and gently stroked her head as he spoke to her in a soothing voice. "I know this is hard, sweetheart. But let me tell you something, just as soon as they deliver your baby, your big ole heart will fill with so much love that you'll think it will burst. And you know what, Betsy? You'll forget all about this pain."

"You've never had a baby! You don't know what this is like. Dad, I can't do this!"

He reached for a wet washcloth and washed her face. "Are you in pain, baby?"

"Not at the moment..."

"Okay. Well, you just tell me when the pain begins. I'll tell you what we're going to do when that pain starts, you squeeze my hand and I'll breathe with you until the contraction stops."

Henry continued to speak in a low and calming voice. "Betsy, you are stronger than you think, sweetheart. God equipped your little body to give birth to this child. Now, girl, you've got to get tough and decide that you and Hal can get through this together."

Betsy looked into her father's eyes and saw the depth of his love for her. Almost within an instant, her body stopped shaking, and she closed her eyes and dozed.

When the next wave of contractions began, Betsy reached for her father's hand, and he talked her through the breathing technique she had learned in the childbirth class. In a few moments, the doctor came in and cleared the room.

It was time. It was time for Betsy to deliver her baby boy.

****

Marsha left and went to the National Guard soldier, who she had spoken to when she first arrived at the cage. She explained her predicament, so he allowed her to go into the cell where Julia was last seen.

She found the dynamics of the cage altogether different from the one she had just come from. First, there were only little boys in this cage, with a sprinkling of a few teenage boys among them. Like the other cage, the kids were all traumatized by the experience they had just endured. Marsha continued to walk around and asked people if they had seen a blonde woman dressed in riding pants and boots. Either no one had seen a woman fitting that description, or they gave her a blank stare and turned their back. Marsha grew frustrated because she was almost at the end of the cage and hadn't yet seen Julia. When she got to the very end, she turned and went back outside.

The soldier standing at the door of the cage gave her a look of concern. Marsha said, "I didn't see her in there anywhere. Is there another area she might have gone to without you seeing her?"

Pointing to the third cage, "Maybe she went in the next one. There will be more adults in there, so be careful."

Marsha expressed her concern about Betsy's appearance of being sedated and unable to stand.

He nodded and said, "Sometimes the guards feel it necessary to sedate them with a shot, especially if they look like they will harm someone." He shrugged his shoulders and said, "I know it sounds barbaric, but, sometimes, it's the only way to maintain order here."

"Well, I've got to figure out a way to get my sister out of that cage."

Marsha headed back toward Betsy. Abruptly, the activity within the cage exploded, as the guards pushed about twenty-five more people inside, and then secured the gate with a crowbar and chain.

As frightened as she was by the commotion, Marsha quickly found her way back to Betsy.

When she returned, she found Betsy had drifted into a sound sleep and was not stirring for anyone. She went through the same routine with her, but to no avail. Supposedly, the fear had escaped her because the uncontrollable shaking had stopped. Marsha just sat next to her for a few minutes until the chaos in the area ended.

A guard came by and looked at Marsha, but she was careful not to make eye contact with him. Instead, she acted as if she was oblivious to his presence in the cell. He moved around from one young girl to another, and Marsha noticed as he pulled something from his backpack. She watched as the guard administered a shot to a little girl who was crying out of control. The little girl fell to the ground, and her head rested on the child sitting next to her.

Chapter Fifty-Six

Isabela moved up to where Julia was sitting in the copilot's seat of the chopper, and watched for Marsha and Julia to return. The longer they were gone, the more anxious Isabela became until she finally jumped to the back of the helicopter.

"Marsha and Julia should be back by now... I'm afraid something has happened to them, so I'm going to get Rod."

Isabela then took off toward the direction where she last saw Rod. She waded through the many people, and finally made her way to his side of the truck. She tugged on his pant leg, and she looked up at him and said, "Marsha and Julia left the chopper to find Betsy, and they aren't back. I got scared and didn't know who else to tell."

Rod dropped down to eye level with Isabela, "it's okay, sweetie. I'll find them. First, tell me where you last saw Julia and Marsha, okay?"

As Rod walked Isabela back to the chopper, he stopped by the holding areas and spoke with a member of the National Guard to explain the situation. The guardsman told him to take the little girl back to the chopper, and he would send over a guy to stand guard.

They discussed organizing a group of six men to go through the bays and look for the three ladies. Rod agreed and picked up little Isabela and ran with her to the chopper, before searching for Julia.

"Isabela, you've got to promise me you will stay here and be brave. I'm going to look for the ladies and will be back in a few minutes."

Tears dripped from Isabela's eyes as she nodded in agreement.

"Listen to me, sweetie," Rod said. "I know you're scared. We all are. But look around at these people here. I don't want you to get lost. Stay here inside the chopper and I promise to come back as soon as I find the ladies. Now give me a high-five for good luck."

Isabela wiped her tears with her hands.

Rod wasn't sure she completely understood everything he said. But she raised her little hand to his, and then she gave his hand a tight squeeze.

****

When he returned, the group of men and Rod went into the first bay, and as they made their way to the back, they found no one in there that fit the description of the two women.

The search intensified as they continued to the other bay areas and buildings looking for the women. Finally, one of the guardsmen spotted Marsha hovering over Betsy in a corner.

As soon as he approached them, he knelt and helped Marsha pick up Betsy, and he slowly swept her up in his arms and led them back to the chopper. As promised, a National Guardsman was standing guard outside the helicopter, keeping an eye on the girls.

Marsha waited outside the chopper while Rod got Betsy comfortable.

"Marsha," Rod asked, "where did Julia go?"

"We separated to look for Betsy. And when I went to tell Julia that I'd found Betsy, then I couldn't find Julia anywhere. Rod, this place is scary."

Rod put his arm around Martha. "I know... I'll be back as soon as I find Julia."

While the men roamed through the last building, he began to panic. Rod had only been to the border a couple times before this visit. Still, he never had a reason to go to the holding areas where the children were left after being separated from their parents. It was an experience he would not soon forget.

The men searching for Julia met outside the last building and regrouped. They reason she had to be in one of the holding areas because the guard watched her enter the second bay.

But where had she gone?

Movement within the holding areas would be easy enough because the petitions between them were unsecured until lockdown late in the day. Rod feared that she, too, had been sedated by one of the guard patrols, especially if she had copped an attitude. Even though he had known her for fewer than twenty-four hours, he knew that it wasn't in her nature to disrespect anyone in an authoritative position.

She was a professional woman. Being raised in a strict home environment, Julia understood the need for rules and regulations.

As the men stood in a circle and discussed a different plan for locating Julia, one guy suggested that they go in pairs to comb the area more thoroughly. With so many children lying around on the floor of the bay, it would be necessary for someone to search the ground while another kept their head up and scanned the faces of the people standing.

They agreed on the plan and paired off before going back inside the bay.

Rod looked at the face of each person he saw in the first holding area, and the thoroughness of the search was time-consuming. He was confident that their efforts would take them to Julia, and he would not leave without her. However, when he realized after searching for two hours, that no one had seen her, he became discouraged. Then, his confidence began to waive.

He went back to the chopper to check on the girls, and Marsha and Betsy wanted to go back with him to help with the search.

"Absolutely not! I need you to stay here and protect these young girls, and besides, you have already tried to help and look where that got you."

Immediately, Rod turned and headed back to the search party, and it was apparent they had gained a second wind. He and his partner bolted into the second bay and continued their search. They were nearing the end of the bay when something caught Rod's attention. He looked back at the area that he had just scanned, and there stood Julia, all alone looking down at the ground. Preoccupied with the young children who sat beneath her. Apparently, Julia had missed seeing Rod and his partner coming through the first time.

Somehow she had found a rubber band and pulled her hair back into a ponytail away from her face, and he didn't recognize her at first glance.

Not knowing if she'd been sedated or was just preoccupied, Rod slowly inched toward Julia until he was standing next to her.

"Hi, pretty lady. What brings you here?" Rod touched her arm. "You look out of place in here with these small children."

Julia was startled, and then she recognized him. She grabbed hold and clung to him for several minutes.

"Thank God, you found me. I've been walking around for what seems like hours looking for Betsy. Then, I must have gotten disoriented because I lost my sense of direction."

"You need some water, young lady. If you were disoriented, it's because of dehydration. Let's get you out of here and find a bottle of water."

She was still clinging to him as they walked through the maze of children, trying not to step on anyone sitting on the floor.

When they reached the entrance, Julia turned to Rod and said, "I've never been so glad to see anyone in my life. Thank you for taking the time to find me."

"Yeah, well. Just so you know, I may never leave your side again."

Julia smiled.

"What do you mean, Rod?"

"When you were missing, my heart ached," Rod said. "I felt sick inside, and then I realized that even though we've just met, I don't ever want us to be apart again."

Julia stood on her tiptoes and pulled his face toward hers and kissed his lips.

"Yep. That's exactly what I thought it would feel like to kiss you."

"And how is that?" Rod winked.

"It was electrifying," Julia said.

Rod wrapped her in his arms and kissed her passionately. The guardsmen who were involved in the search came out and saw the embrace. With fingers between their lips, they began to whistle and shout. Then, they spread high fives among their group and offered congratulatory remarks for a job well done.

Dawkins came over and handed Rod a cooler of food for the girls and congratulated him on his success. Then he leaned in and whispered something in his ear. Rod laughed and then turned and thanked each man personally for taking their time to participate in the search.

As they walked away, Rod reached for Julia's hand, and they walked in the direction of the chopper.

"What did the pilot say," Julia asked, "when he whispered in your ear?"

"You don't want to know."

Julia looked at Rod and rolled her eyes as she shook her head.

When Rod and Julia were in sight of the chopper, the side door opened, and little Isabela jumped to the ground and ran toward them.

She placed her arms around their waist and hugged them both and cried. "I want you to be my mommy and daddy."

Surprised, Rod looked at Julia with raised eyebrows and said, "I'm on board. How about you?"

Julia hugged Isabela and said, "We should be so lucky to have a precious daughter like you."

Chapter Fifty-Seven

Fitz could barely see as he pulled the baseball cap down over his forehead. He walked around the side of the convenience store and dropped to the ground. His ears still rang from the sound of the deafening explosion that destroyed the chopper. Surprised, he couldn't remember how he'd escaped it, but somehow he'd crawled through the escape hatch just in time.

He snuck into the public restroom and washed his face, and then he tried to reach the second in command with the cartel. He needed to get word to the cartel that they'd destroyed the helicopter and tell them about Nic's death.

Fitz knew it would be his responsibility to tell his dying mother that her worst nightmare occurred. He realized she would see right through his explanation and discover his involvement in the family business. A profession he'd promised her he would never take part in.

He listened for movement from the outside, and then he heard the sirens coming from the north. As he opened the restroom door, he saw the pilot sitting in the cockpit, focusing on the preflight checklist. Fitz quickly shut the door and waited.

When he heard the helicopter leave, he opened the restroom door and walked behind the store. But he'd miscalculated the sound of another chopper landing nearby.

A spotlight projected from the aircraft and followed his every move. The loudspeaker announced that he should put his hands behind his head and drop to his knees.

Then, a police car pulled into the parking lot and squealed tires as they applied the brakes. As one deputy secured his wrist, another deputy appeared and pulled him to his feet and frisked him. It was at that precise moment that Fitz knew his life in the cartel was over.

And he wanted it to be over.

As a young boy, he had laid in his bedroom inside their tiny apartment, listening to tales involving the cartel as told to his mother by his Uncle Nic. The stories sounded so glamorous to his young ears. There was talk of high-powered machine guns, helicopters, drugs, and alcohol. And with so much money to keep up with, the family had bought a shrink-wrap machine requiring a uniquely made instrument to penetrate the plastic.

He had grown up dreaming of the day he would become a part of the family business, and the unlimited access to the vast sums of money his uncle had discussed. Little did he know that his mother had forbidden her brother from bringing him into the family cartel. Hence, when he began working for the family business, he told his mother that he had found a magnificent sales job.

However, his former life of lies and deceit was not a lifestyle he now wanted to pursue. He needed to get back to Abington, come clean with his mother before she died, and beg Julia to forgive him for causing her and her family such pain.

He had dated Julia for all the wrong reasons. First, he needed her input in finding skilled help to stay with his mom. Once he found out her dad was sick, and he had a large farm that would be sold upon his death, Fitz started his pursuit. Of course, he was just interested in her because of the land. But once he got to know her, he realized they could make a life together.

While the officer shoved him into the back of the patrol car, he prayed that Julia had loved him, a fact of which he had been unsure.

Chapter Fifty-Eight

A gent Roberts ended the call and looked at Andrew, Rhett, and Laura. They were drinking coffee and eating biscuits at the conference table in Andrew's office.

"Well, the girls are in the air and headed for an undisclosed location for debriefing. We expect this period to last a full twenty-four hours."

Roberts smiled at Laura.

"Your girls will be home around ten o'clock in the morning. May I suggest you all go home and try to get some rest before they arrive. It's been a long couple of days, and I'm sure you could use the rest."

Rhett turned to Laura, "If you like, I'll drive you home."

Laura touched his hand and smiled, "I would like that very much." She then turned back to Agent Roberts, "Is it okay for me to call Hal and Fitz and let them know the girls are now safe and will be home in the morning?"

Roberts looked at Rhett and then to Andrew.

Rhett touched her hand, "Laura, you may want to call Hal as soon as you get home."

"Well, how about Fitz? Julia would want me to contact him, too."

"Honey, he is responsible for Julia and the girls' kidnapping. Fitz is involved in the drug cartel. We didn't tell you earlier, for fear it would upset you. You've been a tower of strength throughout this ordeal."

"Oh, my God!" Laura exclaimed. "Does Julia know this? Has someone told her?"

"We're uncertain how much the girls know at this point," said Roberts. "But we'll soon find out."

They thanked Agent Roberts for his time and efforts. Then Rhett and Laura headed to the farm.

****

As soon as they got home, Laura made a pot of coffee and then went into the study to make the dreaded call to Hal. They spoke for over thirty-minutes as she explained the events of the previous twenty-four hours. At first, it upset Hal that she had not called him sooner. As they continued to talk, he soon understood the logic in not causing the boys to get upset until they knew their mother was safe.

Laura encouraged Hal to be at the house in time to greet Betsy when the chopper landed.

"Laura," said Hal, "should I bring the boys with me tomorrow to meet their mother?"

Laura paused, and considered the delicate state of their marriage, and thought it would be best not to upset the children.

"I think not. If Betsy wants them to know about the kidnapping, she should be able to tell them on her terms, so she can temper the events and not scare them too much."

Laura explained that it's one thing to read about a kidnapping or watch a movie involving the crime. Still, when the abduction includes your own mother, it's a unique situation altogether.

Hal agreed with Laura and told her that he would make some calls and find each of his boys a place to spend the night.

"Hal, you're a smart man," Laura said, "and we love you like our own son. Perhaps we never told you, but we always knew it would take a secure man like you to keep our Betsy happy. She loves you, Hal. But she's going to need some extra attention when she returns. Hopefully, you are in a place to give her the attention she needs."

"You're right. I promise to make Betsy a priority in the future. You have my word, Laura," Hal said. "I'll be there in the morning, around ten o'clock."

When Laura finished the call, Rhett walked into the study with a tray that held coffee and a small plate on which he had placed a sandwich and a few chips. She looked up at his face as he sat the plate on the desk.

"You may very well be the best thing to happen to me in a very long time."

Rhett winked as he handed her a napkin.

"Now, now. Don't get carried away," Rhett said. "I just made a sandwich. I haven't performed espionage or anything."

While Laura ate her sandwich and drank her coffee, Rhett built a fire.

Then they moved to the club chairs in front of the fireplace, and Laura drifted off to sleep. Rhett removed the throw from the sofa, spread it over her body, and then settled back down in the club chair next to her and napped.

When they awoke, it was after four o'clock. As Laura walked toward the master suite, she yelled back at Rhett, "will you be a dear and pour me a drink from the decanter behind the desk, please. Pour you one, too. I'd love to have a drink when I get out of the shower."

Laura enjoyed a long shower and then put on her favorite sweatshirt and leggings. She quickly dried her hair, rubbed moisturizer over her face, and applied a pink-colored lip gloss. Satisfied with the way she looked in the mirror, she then turned and went back into the bedroom, where she found Rhett reading the newspaper.

"Rhett," Laura said, "the bathroom is clean if you want to jump in and take a quick shower."

"Thank you, but I can go home and change."

"Oh, don't be silly. I have a massive walk-in shower here, and there's no need for you to go home now."

"Just one problem. I don't have any clean clothes," Rhett argued.

"No problem." Laura pointed to the master bath. "Go in there and remove your clothes and put on the robe hanging on the back of the door. Then throw me your clothes, and I'll run them through the washing machine and dryer."

He finished the last of his drink.

"I may have some workout clothes in my gym bag in the car that I can wear while you're washing my clothes."

"Well, there you go. That will work." Laura went to the linen closet and removed a large towel and washcloth for him, while Rhett went out to his car to retrieve his gym bag.

When Rhett came back into the master suite, he was smiling.

"What are you smiling about?"

"I can't believe my good fortune. I've found enough clothes in this bag to stay for a week or more! And they're freshly laundered," Rhett said. "There's a pair of sweatpants, a grey t-shirt, a white button-down shirt, and a pair of jeans."

"Well, while you're in the shower, I'll put your clothes in to wash."

****

Rhett stepped through the doorless entrance of the luxurious shower and marveled at the exquisite Italian marble. The area was more spacious than any walk-in closet he'd ever seen. It was so large that they'd positioned the dual shower heads so that the water did not spill out into the adjoining dressing area. As he looked around the shower stall, he laughed at the thought of Henry Whelchel, building such an elaborate place to bathe, and wondered what possessed him to incur that expense.

The warm water from the pulsating showerhead felt invigorating as he lathered himself with the body wash he found in the gym bag. The effect was so relaxing that Rhett allowed it to engulf him as the soap rinsed from his well-toned body.

When he messaged his hair with shampoo, he felt a movement behind him. Startled, Rhett knew he was not alone in the shower. Then, he felt her soft hands rubbing the soapsuds as she pretended to clean his back. Her hands moved with precision as she massaged the tight muscles in his shoulder area.

She whispered in his ear. "I can't believe I'm doing this."

Laura moved closer as he felt her body press against his back. The desire then rose in him as he quickly rinsed the shampoo from his hair. Then he turned toward Laura and saw the wanton look in her eyes as he kissed her with passion…

The next morning, when Laura awoke from a deep, satisfying sleep. She reached over to the other side of the bed, but Rhett was not there. Laura got out of bed and went into the bathroom to brush her teeth and comb her hair. Then she washed her face and applied moisturizer. Her skin felt dry, so she reached for the vitamin E oil, went over, and sat on the bed, and rubbed her arms and legs with the oil.

Rhett came into the bedroom carrying their breakfast. She could tell he had been up for some time because his hair was still damp from his morning shower.

On the tray was a pot of freshly brewed coffee, two plates filled with an omelet, hash brown potatoes, and two slices of buttered toast he had cut diagonally. He had placed a rose from an arrangement she had purchased the previous week in a small crystal vase.

His facial expression told her he was proud of the presentation.

"What are you doing there, sweetheart?" He asked as he positioned the tray on a small table next to the bay window.

"My skin is so dry, and I've been applying oil to my legs."

Rhett poured the coffee, and handed a cup to Laura, as he took the bottle from her hand. As she sipped her morning coffee, Rhett rubbed her feet with the oil.

When he saw that she'd finished the coffee, he removed the cup from her hand and placed it on the small table next to the breakfast tray.

When he looked into her eyes, he saw fresh tears.

"Laura, honey, why are you crying. Is there something wrong?"

Laura reached for a Kleenex and wiped her tears as Rhett looked at her with that adoring smile.

She found something in Rhett that she'd desired for a long time.

Her marriage to Henry was a marriage of convenience, but she'd always yearned for something more. She wanted to be with a man that adored her and wanted to spend each moment together.

She craved genuine love. The kind that aches in your heart when you're apart.

Laura had compromised her own feelings for Henry, but when she met Rhett, he sparked something inside her that she had never experienced or had never known existed.

"No, Rhett, these are tears of joy. I haven't felt this way in such an awfully long time. And to be honest, I never expected to feel this way again. When Henry died, I thought any joy in my life was about over."

He lifted the strand of hair and kissed the abrasion over her eye. Rhett paused and stared at her with those adoring eyes.

"No, babe, we're just getting started."

He winked at her as his lips evoked feelings she'd never known.

Then with a mischievous look and a gentle movement, Rhett rolled Laura onto her stomach. She giggled as he began to rub the oil on the back of her body. And, again, they were overcome by their desire...

Chapter Fifty-Nine

R od received the flight instructions when he and the girls were on board the helicopter and ready to take off. He looked at his phone and then looked around for his bearings, "Ladies, we are about to leave, so please fasten your seat belts. After we are in the air, you will find sandwiches and drinks in the cooler. Help yourself. When we arrive at our destination at 1500 hours, you will soon begin the debriefing process. I'm sure you'll receive a hot meal and have an opportunity to shower before lights out at 2200 hours. Unless we hear otherwise, I will fly you to Abington first thing in the morning. So, sit back and enjoy the ride."

Julia was sleeping when Rod gained clearance to land the chopper at the Dobbins Air Reserve Base in Marietta, Georgia. The other girls exited the aircraft and followed the Staff Sergeant to the main building at the base. As he watched the others walk away from the helicopter, Rod reached over and woke Julia from a sound sleep, with a gentle nudge.

"Where are we?"

"We've just landed at Dobbins. The girls have gone ahead, but I wanted to talk with you a minute before you go in. We may not have an opportunity to talk again until we fly to Abington in the morning."

She smiled as she noticed the concern in his eyes. They talked for a while longer, and Rod told Julia that he was serious when he told Isabela that he would adopt her.

"Rod, you can't be serious! She's just a little girl who was freaked out at the time. She didn't realize what she was asking of us."

They'd talked for over an hour when he received a text. He chuckled, "Well, times up, it looks like your interview with me is over. Now it's time for your formal debriefing. I'll go in with you, and depending on who is in charge, it may work out for us to get together later in the evening. I'd really like to continue our conversation."

After the debriefing, the C.O. in charge looked at Rod and said, "Listen, you need to stand guard at the door while your wife showers and gets changed. Then take her down to the mess hall and get her some grub. Don't leave her side. If you like, your daughter can join you in the mess hall while you're eating dinner. The others have two guards directing their every move, and I can't afford for your wife to be alone. I know it's a pain, but it's part of the debriefing protocol."

Rod agreed to stay with Julia through each step of the process.

As they were leaving the room, he turned to the C.O. and asked, "where are we to sleep?"

The C.O. looked at his pad and said, "We only have two beds available tonight, but the others are all staying in the same room. We can have a cot moved in for your daughter, or would you prefer to be alone tonight?"

Rod glanced at Julia, "Thank you, sir. We appreciate it."

Julia and Rod walked around the barracks after dinner and found the room where the others were staying. But they weren't in there. They were already meeting with counselors about their experience with the kidnappers and their time at the border.

Rod suggested they check out their own room before it was Julia's turn to meet with a counselor. As they walked in the door, they noticed the sparse accommodations. There were two cots and a nightstand. A lamp was lit as if someone had been in there to prepare their room. Rod noticed the clean sheets were folded military style, complete with a crisp corner. There was a pillow, and a dark, grey blanket someone had folded across the foot of the bed. Under the window sat a small table which served as a desk, and a single chair. The apportionment of the room was scarce. However, they would be there less than twenty-four hours, and they just needed a place to lay their heads for a few hours before the FBI released them for home.

Julia watched as Rod closed the door behind them.

"You should have told him the truth about us not being married, and that Isabela isn't our daughter," Julia said. "I feel bad that we are so deceitful."

"Well, if I'd told him the truth, he would have placed us in separate rooms. Or you'd be down there with the other girls, and I'd be up here all alone."

Julia sat on the bed and looked around the room.

"Rod, you can't be serious about what Isabela asked of us, can you? You realize she was scared to death at the time and she was just searching for an answer."

He walked over to the window and looked at the sunset. As he watched the dark blue, purple, and pink colors change to black, he thought I *can only imagine the fear those young girls felt when they were separated and placed in foster homes. Once again, fear must have been horrific when they walked into that big trailer, with no idea what their future held.*

He turned around and smiled at Julia.

"Actually, Julia, I am dead serious. I don't understand why you helped save those girls if you had no intention of creating a better life for them. You said yourself that you came from a close-knit family, and judging from your father's occupation, you weren't poor."

Julia became defensive and started rambling on about it being Marsha's idea to save the girls in the first place. She admitted that she'd never really given much thought to what they would do with them once they got back home.

Rod was quick to point out that Marsha told the girls, in his presence, that their home was now in Abington.

Their argument continued until they called Julia back to finish her debriefing. Rod walked with her down to the room and sat outside the door while she completed the interrogation.

The C.O. walked by and told Rod that he would be off duty soon, but he hoped they found their accommodations acceptable.

The debriefing lasted almost two hours, and when she exited the room, Julia's eyes were red and puffy. Considering she had briefly napped a few times throughout the past couple of days, she felt physical and mental exhaustion. Rod reached for her arm, and they tiptoed back to the assigned room.

When Rod opened the door, he noticed someone had turned on the lamp. He smiled when he discovered a bottle of champagne in a bucket of ice on the desk and two small plastic cups. "This is a nice touch."

"Rod, did you do this for me?"

"No. I didn't. But I must admit, someone had a great idea." He touched her arm, "I know you're tired and ready for bed, but do you feel like having a glass of champagne with me before you go to sleep?"

After Rod opened the bottle, he filled the glasses and handed one to Julia. He looked into her eyes and said, "You've lived through a few tough days, my dear. I admire your courage."

"Thank you."

As he sipped his champagne, he remembered a conversation with his mom about knowing in an instant when he met the woman of his dreams.

I've known a few women in my life, but I'm sure that Julia's the one for me.

"We can adopt Isabela or not. It's your call. But I know one thing, I want to wake up each morning with you by my side, and I want to kiss you each night before I go to sleep."

"You don't even know me!"

"Yes, I do," Rod said. "I know enough."

This relationship was moving much faster than he'd expected. But he wasn't backing down. He had never felt this way about another person, and he wasn't about to let her get away.

"Okay, then. Tell me five things you know about me?"

Rod sat down in the chair. He crossed his arms and looked up at the ceiling. He made a face like he was trying hard to think of something to say.

"There you go! You can't even name five things you know about me," Julia said. "And you're ready to move in together and raise a young girl. A young girl whose culture differs completely from anything we know."

Rod got up from the chair and walked toward her.

"I know you're smart and courageous. You're willing to take a chance on someone you believe in, and you have tenacity. And oh, yeah, you're a good kisser."

"So, does this mean you're asking me to marry you?"

Rod sipped from his glass and smiled. "Well, since you mentioned it, yes, I would like to marry you."

Then he gently took the glass from her hand as he looked into her eyes.

Several seconds passed. Embarrassed, Julia looked at the ground and laughed.

"Rod, this is when you're supposed to kiss me."

"I thought you'd never ask."

He smiled as he wrapped her in his arms and kissed her with a passion she had never known.

Chapter Sixty

The agent helped Fitz into the chopper, and they headed toward Atlanta. When they were about to land at the private airport, Fitz asked if they would take him on to Abington before they turned him over to the authorities. He explained his need to go to the hospital to sign over a power of attorney for his sick mother, and if they had time, he needed to go by the Whelchel farm.

They radioed ahead and got permission.

There was a car waiting at the small airport in Abington. Fitz and the FBI agent got into the car, and the driver asked the destination.

When the agent nodded at Fitz, he said, "The Medical Center, please."

As they pulled up to the portico at the emergency entrance, Fitz held his breath as he looked down at his hands.

How will I ever find the words to tell my sweet mother that I went against her wishes and worked for her Colombian family? How often did I hear her ask Uncle Nic to keep me away from the corrupt cartel life?

"Sir, we're here. My agent will go in with you to visit your mother. He'll wait outside the door to her room. You have thirty minutes, and then we must leave."

Fitz's movements lacked energy. Although his hands remained in cuffs, he stepped outside the car without assistance. Together, he and the agent entered the hospital and took the elevator to the I.C.U. When he looked into her unit, he noticed something was wrong. They had stripped the hospital bed, and a junior staffer was busy wiping it down with an alcohol wipe.

As he walked into the vacant room, the head nurse rushed over to him.

"Fitz, is that correct?"

Fitz covered his face and nodded.

"Sir, I'm so sorry. Please come and sit a moment. We need to talk."

The nurse directed him across the room to a small sofa, and motioned for him to sit. She leaned back against the windowsill as she removed the envelope from the pocket of her uniform.

"May I call you Fitz?"

"What? Excuse me, yes. Of course."

"Fitz, your mom passed away about an hour ago. When you last saw your mother, she was in a comatose state. Her body kept retaining water, and as hard as we tried, we could not keep the fluid from building up in her lungs... You knew she had congestive heart failure, right?"

Fitz nodded.

"Well, your mom regained consciousness yesterday morning for a few minutes, and we tried to contact you. When she realized that you were away on family business, she asked me to make sure you received this envelope."

Fitz reached for the envelope. He stared at the initials, as he recognized the beautiful script of his mother's handwriting. He lifted the envelope to his face and covered his eyes.

The nurse patted his shoulder and said, "I'm going back out to the nurse's station to give you a few moments alone. You'll find your mother's belongings in the bag next to the chair. Let me know if you need anything."

Slumping in his seat, he opened the envelope and removed the single piece of paper on which she had written:

My dearest Fitz,

I'm sorry I missed saying goodbye to you, my son. My body has just worn out, and I know my time here on earth is ending. Please remember that you are, and always have been, the light of my world. How I wish that we had more time together. There are things I need to tell you. Perhaps there are things you need to say to me, as well.

As I leave this world, please understand that all I ever wanted for you was a good, clean, respectable life. I hope you find that life someday. Often the consequences of our decisions are painful and lasting. Make sure you choose good over evil, and always choose love!

With all my heart, I love you, son!

Mamá

When they pulled onto Whelchel road, Fitz asked the driver to go around to the back driveway because he didn't want to alarm anyone. He had overheard on the radio during the flight that the girls would return home around five o'clock. When Fitz looked at his watch, the aircraft was on time, and his heart raced as he thought of what he would say to Julia after she returned home. He was grateful that Julia and her family had welcomed his mother into their home. Now he would need to apologize to them for his actions of the past month, and ask for their forgiveness.

The helicopter landed, and Fitz watched as Betsy, Marsha, and some other girl exited the chopper. Then, he saw Julia, and there was an intimate familiarity in the way the pilot touched her that caused him to pause. The pilot then reached for the hand of one of the younger girls. Fitz noticed the girl standing next to Julia looked toward him, then looked up at Julia and said something. Julia looked in his direction and then glanced away as the pilot reached for her hand, and made a comment that caused her to laugh.

Fitz turned to the agent standing next to him, "Thank you, sir. I need not speak with her after all. I'm ready to go."

Chapter Sixty-One

Rhett was wearing a pair of well-fitted, dark-colored jeans, and a white button-down shirt with the sleeves rolled up half-way. He looked at his phone as he walked outside to the car. He placed the gym bag in the trunk, and as he closed it, he heard the helicopter coming in the distance.

He stuck his head in the door and said, "Laura, the chopper is headed this way!"

Laura's face was aglow as she walked outside the house wearing a pair of white jeans, a faded blue jean jacket, with a white camisole underneath. With just enough time to shower, she had little time to style her hair, so she added a generous amount of mousse and let it dry naturally. The sun dried, beach effect of her blonde hair made her look younger than her sixty-three years. Rhett smiled with admiration as he watched her walk down the steps.

"You know, you look way too young to have three grown daughters." He kissed her forehead, as he placed his arm around her waist. They watched as the chopper landed. Rhett reached for her hand when the rotors stopped, and they walked toward the field across the road.

Hal skidded into the driveway just in time to watch Betsy appear in the aircraft's doorway. A huge smile appeared on her face when she saw Hal jump out of the car and sprint across the road to the helicopter. She slowly made her way down the steps and stopped as Hal picked her up and swung her around like he hadn't seen her in months. When he set her on the ground, he took her face in his hands and looked into her eyes, and then he gave her a sweet kiss.

"Well, perhaps I should run off more often," Betsy say. "This is an amazing homecoming for me."

"Oh, no," he said. "Today, we're starting a new chapter in our lives. On the way over here this morning, it occurred to me that love requires action, and I plan to spend the rest of my life showing you how much you mean to me."

****

As Laura and Rhett watched the girls exit the chopper, Laura asked, "Why are they wearing army fatigues, Rhett?"

"Perhaps they went to a military base for the debriefing."

Marsha was the next one to exit the plane, and in a true dramatic style, she turned and saluted the pilot, then waved and blew a kiss to her mother. Rhett immediately recognized her resemblance to Henry with her beautiful olive complexion and dark brown hair. She was tall and willowy compared to Betsy's petite frame.

Then, three beautiful, Hispanic girls appeared at the door of the chopper, and Laura looked at Rhett and said, "Who are those children?"

He squeezed her waist and said, "I don't know, Laura, but I'm sure we're about to find out."

The pilot moved around the young girls and held out his hand for the older child, assisting her down the steps. He climbed back up the steps and picked up the other two girls and brought them down.

As soon as Julia appeared on the landing, Rhett noticed Laura's resemblance.

Gosh, Julia's gorgeous. Laura must have looked just like Julia at that age. No wonder Henry didn't involve Laura in our meetings. He was keeping her to himself.

The pilot turned toward Julia, smiling as he reached for her hand. He held it until she was safely on the ground as if she were royalty descending to an imaginary red carpet.

****

As Julia walked down the steps of the helicopter, she noticed a man standing to the side of a black SUV near the entrance to the rear-drive. Although the guy was in handcuffs, she recognized the aviator shades and the black baseball cap he was wearing. For once, she was unaffected by the sight of Fitz Romano, and felt no remorse for his current situation.

Julia turned back around as Rod reached for Isabela's hand.

"I've been thinking about our discussion last night," Julia said.

"And?" Rod replied.

"My answer is yes."

Rod took her hand while he kissed the top of her forehead.

"I knew you'd say yes."

Then the three of them walked across the road.

Laura cried as she hugged her daughters. There were hugs all around from Laura as she introduced Rhett to each of the girls.

Then Marsha placed her arms around Maria, Isabela, and Lucia and introduced them to Laura and Rhett.

"I know this is hard to believe, Mom, but these girls have changed us. They have taught us so much about life, and have shown us the true meaning of unconditional love. We hope you guys will also come to love them."

Chapter Sixty-Two

When the chatter stopped, the silence was almost deafening as time stood still. Laura felt a calm had returned to her existence as she looked at her girls and Rhett, knowing that amid her darkest hour, she'd found the man who'd given her the gift of pure joy.

After processing what Marsha said, she realized the events of the last few days had been life-changing for her girls, too. They had left home selfish and entitled. However, they'd gained a certain level of empathy for humanity along their journey. A character trait Henry had spent a lifetime trying to instill.

Laura noticed that Rhett's eyes had filled with tears, as he nodded toward the younger girls, both of whom were looking up at her with the most beautiful black eyes. There was something about the sight of the young girls that grabbed at his heart. His face told her he'd resisted the urge to take the little girls in his arms and assure them of their safety.

Then Laura remembered something that Henry said many years ago.

Rhett blames himself for his wife's death and the baby girl they lost during childbirth. He's spent all these many years, trying to reconcile this with himself.

Rhett touched her elbow as his voice cracked. "Honey, they look like they could use some attention, too."

Together they stooped down in front of the little Hispanic girls. With tears in her eyes and a grateful heart, Laura said, "Welcome home, my little Princesas!"

****

The emotions of seeing her mother again caused Julia to wipe the tears from her face. Then she felt a soft hand pull at her own, and she looked down at Isabela's beautiful face.

"Who is that man standing next to the truck over near the woods?"

"He's just someone I used to know," Julia said. "But those ties are now broken."

Isabela looked confused.

Julia smiled wistfully as she watched her mother and Rhett whisper among themselves. There was a sense of bliss on her mother's face that she had never seen. Then, she realized that this handsome man had given her mother a new lease on life.

As she lifted her head, Julia looked out over the farm she loved. "Isabela, a wise woman once said that life-altering decisions are often made in a split second, but broken ties can last forever."

The End

ABOUT THE STORY

Fractured-A Story of Broken Ties is a work of fiction, and any similarities to real incidences are coincidental.

The proximity of her hometown to the Hartsville-Jackson International Airport, and the increased advent of sex trafficking in our country prompted this story. It is Renee's intention to raise awareness among the young women of her community.

Estimates suggest that about 50,000 people are trafficked into the US each year, most often from Mexico and the Philippines. This statistic does not include the number of children in the US trafficked by their own family members or neighbors.

Renee encourages anyone who notices another human being in what looks like an unusual or distressed situation to contact The National Human Trafficking Hotline 1.888.373.7888. SMS 233733 (Text "HELP" or "INFO") 24 hours a day, seven days a week. Humantraffickinghotline.org. Or contact the authorities in your area.

Your phone call may save a life!

ABOUT THE AUTHOR

Renee Propes lives in Gainesville, Georgia, with her husband, Hardy, and their Yorkshire Terrier, Lucy. Renee and Hardy have one son, Zachary, and a daughter-in-law, Katie.

Books by Renee Propes

Duplicity – A Story of Deadly Intent
Fractured – A Story of Broken Ties

authorreneepropes.com
rlpropes@bellsouth.net
rpropes17@icloud.com

Acknowledgments

Fractured-A Story of Broken Ties is the second book in the Abington Series. I particularly enjoyed blending characters from Duplicity and introducing new members of the Abington Community.

Thanks to Mitchelle Johnson and Trisha Covin for reading the original unedited draft. I am grateful for your honest assessment, which prompted vast improvements to the story.

A heartfelt thank you to Jane Green Truelove, of J. Green Salon for her endorsement of my first book. Jane, along with her staff, Joan Anderson, Vicki Bobby, Sandy Booth, Callie Hubbard, Wendy Parks, and Rita Wilson, have proven to be the best marketing team around. J. Green Salon is now the official "beauty shop" of Abington, Georgia.

Elizabeth Jones Waidelich, my treasured friend, edited and provided guidance for Fractured. A great big thank you to Liz, for her investment in the Abington series.

Thanks to Rosemary O'Keefe, Deborah Jones-Smith, Martha Megahee, Jean Ellis, and Mary Ellen Prater for the generosity extended in reading the manuscript prior to submission. Thanks for the time and energy you gave to this project. I cannot thank you enough.

Many thanks to Dr. Sidney Washington for his time clarifying medical terminology and research regarding military maneuvers. I'm also grateful to Sidney for the many manuscript proofs.

To our friend and local attorney, William (Bill) Hardman, for his contribution to the courtroom scene involving the trial of "Little Jimmy" Levinson. Thank you, Bill!

Special thanks to Julie Winslett for her friendship and encouragement throughout the writing of this book.

To Grace Wynter, for her editing. Thank you, Grace, for your friendship.

A special thank you to my publishers at the Kimmer Group, for once again guiding me through this arduous process. You guys rock!

I would be remiss if I did not thank the many people in my community and throughout the nation who have supported me on this journey.

A special thanks to my family, Hardy, Zach, Katie, and our fur babies, Lucy and Ollie. Everything begins and ends with you guys.

Above all, to my sweet friend, Jesus, for making this book possible!

CPSIA information can be obtained
at www.ICGtesting.com
Printed in the USA
LVHW082232081021
699965LV00003B/84/J